BLACK REVOLUTIONARIES ON CHICAGO'S WEST SIDE

BLACK REVOLUTIONARIES ON CHICAGO'S WEST SIDE

A History of the Illinois Black Panther Party

Jon F. Rice

Historical Preservation Society Press

Chicago

Black Revolutionaries on Chicago's West Side:
A History of the Illinois Black Panther Party

First Historical Preservation Society Press edition, 2026
Originally published in 1998 as a doctoral dissertation.

This edition prepared for publication by Leila Wills.

Published by
Historical Preservation Society Press
Chicago, Illinois

Distributed by Ingram Content Group

ISBN 979-8-9950089-3-4 (hardcover)
ISBN 979-8-9950089-4-1 (paperback)
ISBN 979-8-9950089-5-8 (epub)

Library of Congress Control Number: 2026937884

Book design by Leila Wills
Cover image: Chicago History Museum, ICHi-076562; Stephen Deutch,
photographer

Printed in the United States of America

10 9 8 7 6 5 4 3 2 1

This 1998 dissertation looks at an historical episode in the history of a people. The people are black migrants from the U.S. South; the setting is the West Side of Chicago.

Contents

Introduction

Just thirty-five years ago, Harold Gosnell's *Negro Politicians*, published in 1935, was one of few monographs on black Chicago politics. Scholarly literature on black Chicago included Gosnell's book, along with Horace Cayton and St. Clair Drake's *Black Metropolis* (1945). By the 1960s, Allan Spear's *Black Chicago* (1969) and Arvarh Strickland's *History of the Chicago Urban League* (1966) had also been written. With the new social history interest in local studies, James Grossman studied the great migration of blacks to Chicago in the early twentieth century in *Land of Hope*, published in 1989. Arnold Hirsch studied the ghettoization process in Chicago, *Making the Second Ghetto* (1985), and non-professional Dempsey Travis wrote three historical impressions of post-World War II, black Chicago, including *An Autobiography of Black Chicago* (1983). More recently, Mitchell Duneier produced a study of working-class blacks on Chicago's South Side entitled *Slim's Table* (1992).

Since the election of Harold Washington as Chicago's first black mayor in 1983, there have been several books on him and his election, including Melvin Holli and Paul Green (1987) and William Grimshaw (1992). Both of these books mention the assassination of Fred Hampton, Chairman of the Illinois Black Panther Party, as a catalyst in the movement that put Harold Washington in office. However, there is nothing in the historiography of black Chicago about a tradition of black radical politics, except a dissertation written by Christopher Reed in 1982. Reed briefly explored the National Negro Congress, which was organized in Chicago in the late 1930s. So this dissertation is perhaps the first full study of black radicals in Chicago. Oppressive living conditions in a time of social fluidity and rising expectations (i.e., the Civil Rights

Movement of the 1960s in a black Chicago slum) might produce a revolutionary group dedicated to radical change. A few monographs explain the poor living conditions of Chicago's South Side ghetto and its lack of community-controlled politicians. No studies discuss the West Side ghetto, however, and its living conditions and lack of political representation. James Grimshaw's Bitter Fruit (1992) explains the failure of the Democratic Party to address the needs of the black community. Grimshaw mentions that the black West Side is ruthlessly oppressed by corrupt, Mafia-connected politicians and that its citizenry is unable to mount an independent movement.[1]

The opening chapter of this study explores the revolutionary predecessors to the Black Panther Party, the Communist Party in black Chicago of the 1930s. The 500 or so blacks who joined the Communist Party in the 1930s and the reception they received from the political establishment and from the black community give a hint of what would later become of the Black Panther Party in Chicago. It also gives a glimpse of the character of law enforcement in the black community and of how Chicago's black community might regard, and accept or reject, revolutionary thought.

Alphine Jefferson's dissertation, "Housing Discrimination and Community Response in North Lawndale," (1979) stands alone, however, in documenting the ghettoization of one West Side community, North Lawndale, as it turned from largely Jewish to black, between the years 1948 and 1960. No other historical or political study focuses on the black West Side of Chicago, which includes the communities of North Lawndale, East and West Garfield and the Near West Side (known to the residents as Miles Square). The second chapter here is a look at these communities in the 1960s and at the political spirit that grew out of their fight with the notorious West Side bloc–a cabal of politicians who controlled politics on the West Side.

The 1960s witnessed the end of the Second Great Migration of rural southern black Americans to urban centers of the north. In Chicago, some 180,000 migrants came and settled on the city's West Side, where immigrants before them had come and settled, many of whom refused to allow participation in the political and economic life of the city to these new "immigrants." This chapter, and beyond, is about these people. They were an unrepresented, economically impoverished people, and their community was ready to fight. When the Student Nonviolent Coordinating Committee (SNCC) came to the West Side in 1968, with the tactics of mass-line, which they had developed in rural Mississippi and Alabama, they walked into a fertile political field. That they came in under the influence, and using the rhetoric of Mao Tse-tung and Algerian revolutionary Frantz Fanon meant that they would attract the attention of the national as well as the local government. This history attempts to explain how the political struggle that radicals and the political establishment waged was played out, and what its effect was on Chicago's West Side.

The life of the black community on the West Side of Chicago has not been portrayed on a historical level.[2] The spirit, the vibrancy, the rage at conditions, the optimism of that culture, in this post-war period, or any other time for that matter, has been skipped over. Often, black histories focus either on black individuals' achievements in spite of the odds or on the victimization of the community as a whole. However, this study is about the culture as the protagonist, and about the cultural experiences during the time in which it was still southern rural but becoming northern urban. The nature of this study differs from that of other studies in that it focuses on the community and the activists who are products of that community. This is a community in which the elected leaders did not represent the interests of the community, either because that leadership was not of the community, or had been intimidated or bought out. This community can be characterized as having an unofficial political leadership of its own. Miles Square was the first and only successful home of the Illinois Black Panther Party, the only black-run revolutionary party in the history of the United States. How that revolutionary spirit took hold in this community, and the peculiar character that the Illinois Black Panther Party had, which set it apart from other Black Panther chapters in other cities, is explored in Chapter 4. The chapter further explores the philosophy and actions of the Panther Party. It explores the difference between the Panthers and the Communists. The homegrown Panther revolutionary philosophy, which began with Marx, ended up more like the International Workers of the World, the "Wobblies."

Interviews were the main sources for characterizing the Illinois Black Panther Party in this study. What they said about themselves, what others said about them, and how they were perceived by the author are the basis for characterizing them in this study. Having interviewed several police officers, as well as a dozen community activists of the late 1960s, I found it surprising that there was such unanimity about the Illinois Black Panther Party. In the past few years, three books on the Black Panther

Party have been published, centering on the groups fountainhead and founder, Huey P. Newton. But this Chicago story is not centered on the Illinois Panther Party's charismatic leader, Fred Hampton, but on the people in and around the Panthers, and the circumstances of this particular urban political environment. It is further about how the police department and the Illinois Panthers were manipulated into violent confrontations. Chapter 5 explores the police and the Panther/police violence.

On election day, April 10, 1928, Octavius Granady, a locally well-known black lawyer, was doing some independent electioneering in the 20th Ward (the Near West Side). Granady was in his car, parked on 1222 S. Blue Island Avenue, when a police car with four police officers pulled up alongside Granady. Several witnesses said the police officers opened fire on Granady, without provocation, in broad daylight, then chased the car for several blocks, firing at the driver. Granady was killed, and his driver, Euclid Taylor, was critically wounded. In this assassination, there is evidence concerning why the six black aldermen in Chicago's City Council of the 1960s never addressed the issues of housing, jobs and city services, three issues of central concern to the black community. The assassination also flavored the type of independent politics that would exist in black Chicago. Forty years after Granady was killed by police, another police-executed assassination took place, and its victim was the chairman of the Illinois Black Panther Party. Chapter 6 explores the nature of the police versus the Panthers in an attempt to understand the latter assassination.

The Black Panther Party was openly anti-government, which was a political stance that invited investigation by the federal government. The nature of the government's policy toward domestic revolutionaries determined how the Black Panther Party was handled on a federal level. A look at the Panther Party in Chicago, therefore, explores how the federal government involved itself in local Chicago politics. Studying the West Side of black Chicago in the 1960s examines a time and a place in which the local people are not represented in the local politics. This study explains how the system that excluded them was maintained and what their more radical responses were to that politically repressive situation. So this is not a study of the Panther phenomenon as much as it is a study of black Chicago. The Black Panther Party originated in Oakland, California, or in Lowndes County, Alabama, depending on how you look at that phenomenon, and there are other studies on these origins.[3]

Notes

1. James Grimshaw, *Bitter Fruit: Black Politics and the Chicago Machine, 1931–1991* (Chicago: University of Chicago Press, 1992), 120.
2. With the exception of Alphine Jefferson's dissertation.
3. There are at least seven books on the Black Panther Party that center on Huey P. Newton and the Oakland headquarters of the Party. Clayborne Carson's *In Struggle* describes the birth of the Black Panther Party in Alabama.

Chapter 1

Predecessors to the Black Panthers: Black Communists in Chicago, 1930-1960

Black Chicagoans elected the first black U.S. Representative of the twentieth century. Oscar DePriest, a Republican, was a believer in capitalism. He made money off Chicago's dual-housing market, raising the rent on his buildings as the residents changed from white to black renters.[1] Segregated housing was big money in Chicago, and someone was going to make that money, so why not him? That was DePriest's argument, and most of the people in the community apparently did not begrudge him for it. DePriest was opposed to government interference in social issues. He was a Hoover man in the decade of the 1920s, advocating self-help and volunteerism, opposing communism.[2]

DePriest's political power, on a national level, was largely symbolic. He was the only black in an avidly racist Congress. DePriest was a fighter. He fought for the right to be served in a Washington, D.C. restaurant where other Representatives ate. In Congress, he fought verbal battles with Southern Democrats on behalf of black people in America. He sponsored an anti-lynching bill.[3] His community admired him for his aggressive stance. However, DePriest did not fight for better conditions in his own district, nor did that black Chicago community of the 1920s demand that of him.

DePriest had a power base. He had the financial backing of moneyed people in the black community: Banker Jesse Binga, and allegedly, the big "policy" wheels (gamblers who controlled the then-illegal lottery), Dan "Mushmouth" Johnson and Dan Jackson, all supported DePriest financially.[4]

These gamblers were the richest men in a segregated, heavily discriminated-against community, and so, reportedly, were more community-minded than comparable white gamblers. They had a spirit that went with the racial oppression of that era.[5] They were committed to a community that was 100,000 people, largely poor (about 5 percent middle class),[6] surrounded by an openly racist population of three million–though, of course, all whites were not actively racist. Still, the 1919 race riot, in which Irish gangs raided the black community in cars, heavily armed, shooting at everyone and where gangs of whites, of integrated ethnicities, attacked black-owned homes outside that ghetto, increased the besieged mentality within that ghetto.[7]

To increase that isolation further, the Irish gangs had evidently painted themselves in black-face and raided the Slavic community to their south and west, and burned several homes there. We can either believe that, or believe somehow a gang of black men, late at night, made it through Irish Bridgeport--without retaliating on the Irish--and got into the Slavic community to wreak havoc there. Motives point the other way. The more recent immigrant Slavs tended to vote a Labor Party ticket, blacks voted Republican, and the Irish voted Democratic. An alliance between Slavs and blacks could have unseated the Democratic-run city government.[8]

The black ghetto residents lived under a state of siege. From 1917 through 1921, there were some seventy-three bombings of black homes at the edge of the black ghetto, as it expanded into white areas; no bombers were ever convicted.[9] Bombings of black-owned homes bought in white communities did not cease until the early sixties. There were restrictive covenants in the surrounding communities that prevented white homeowners from selling their homes to blacks.[10] There were segregated schools and gerrymandered school districts to preserve racial segregation.[11] Numerous private companies refused to hire blacks.[12]

Race mattered, and from within the ghetto, it was a paramount consideration. In that social atmosphere of intense segregation in housing, employment opportunities and educational opportunities, it is obvious that political coalition building, across ethnic lines, was not a political option for black people to initiate.

The Great Depression of the 1930s, which caused business failures and unemployment all across the nation, was particularly hard on a black Chicago ghetto that had begun to grow in economic power. The thriving but small black businesses operating in the black business district, which ran along State Street, from 31st to 39th Streets, almost all succumbed to the hard times. The Binga State Bank and the Frederick Douglass Bank (the first and only black-owned banks in Illinois) closed by 1933, costing thousands of black investors all their savings.[13]

The rise of a Chicago political machine, and the growth of its power and money in Chicago's city government, came at the same time as the failure of the Binga State Bank and the deepening of poverty in the black community. The black community had more than doubled in population over that ten-year span of the 1920s, was more crowded, and politically and financially less powerful.[14] Politicians could ignore the black community more easily in 1930 than in 1920 due to its lack of an independent financial base, where political independence tends to be born. Moreover, where a political machine is present, economic impotence translates into political peonage.[15] The Depression virtually destroyed political independence in Chicago's black community.

Social Conditions

The number one social issue in the black community in the 1930s and 1940s was housing. The doubling of the black population in ten years was not accompanied by much increase in the geographic area the black ghetto occupied. A place to live was hard to find. As a result, rent was often double the rate of white residents only a block away.[16] Unemployment in the black community had risen to more than 50 percent by 1930.[17] There were consequently quite a few people unable to pay their rent. Evictions became an increasingly frequent phenomenon, and the more common they became, the more insecure the people became in that ghetto.[18] Families were facing evictions, usually by absentee landlords. Black families began building shacks. Single men by the hundreds moved into Washington Park and set up tents.[19]

Population density in the black ghetto of Chicago was 70,000 people per square mile, compared to 30,000 in the crowded white community of Kenwood, just south of the ghetto.[20] To give an idea of just how intensely hemmed in that black ghetto was, is as if the population density of that ghetto had occurred all over Chicago, the city would have had a population of thirty-two million rather than just more than three million.[21]

RADICALS OF THE 1930S AND 1940S

While black Republicans were deciding *if* they should address the needs of their community, a new political group was addressing these needs. They were the Communists, and communism was a bad word in mainstream politics in the 1920s. They were, however, the only political group that reached out to Chicago's black community.

It was in the spring of 1931 that the Communist Party began to "unevict" evicted tenants on the black South Side, taking the furniture that the landlord had had put out on the street and putting it back into their apartments. By that summer, thousands of neighbors had joined in to halt the scores of evictions being carried out each month.

Hundreds of evictions were stopped by a community, described in the press as "angry and desperate."[22]

On August 3, 1931, the police were sent to 51st and Dearborn Streets to stop citizens from moving 78-year-old Dianna Gross back into her apartment. There were thousands of people present when the police arrived, and their response was defiant.[23] A fight erupted between the police and the crowd, and the officers fired into the crowd, killing three young men. Whether the police were attacked before or after the shooting is disputed, but at least three police officers were injured.[24] Sydney Jones, a young man at the time, described the event as involving the entire community. He said he was not aware at the time that the Communists were involved. He was knocked unconscious during the fighting, and several other people were injured.[25]

The killings provoked the entire community, and just as significantly, those killings aroused the white working-class areas just west of the ghetto, also the largely Slavic Back-of-the-Yards. In a giant funeral procession described as anywhere from 15,000 to 110,000 strong, and about 25 percent white, the bodies of two of the slain men were carried downtown, past Mayor Cermak's office.[26] Mayor Cermak subsequently issued a suspension of evictions. Black Chicagoans attempting to ameliorate the conditions in their community were often in the Communist Party. Many of them were from the recently defunct United Negro Improvement Association of Marcus Garvey. From the black nationalist movement to a world proletariat movement, these blacks evidently wanted an organization that was primarily sincere about helping their community, whatever its ideology.[27]

Over the next few years, the Communists picked up some 500 black members out of its 2,000 total members in Chicago.[28] By their success, the Communists pushed the Democratic Party and the local branch of the NAACP to become more involved in the serious housing and job issues in the black ghetto.[29]

After the unrest of the summer of 1931, the police developed another way of handling radicals. They ignored the people on the street, at the rallies, and targeted selected Communists. They then raided the local office of the Communist Party and beat them out of the sight of the public. These beatings became so frequent and so brutal that a prerequisite for being a Communist leader was a big, muscular body and a fearlessness toward police.[30] Black Communist Harry Haywood relates that one Communist, Lee Mason, was killed by police[31] and another died of his beating two years later. The press confirmed the latter death.[32]

Most, if not all, of this history has been ignored by historians of Chicago. Historians have not recorded the radicalism in the black community before the 1960s. Yet this radicalism involved some of the most talented men and women in the black community. Radical activists in the Communist Party included Brown Squire, who ran for state office in 1932; political activists and writers Claude Lightfoot, attorney William Patterson, novelist Richard Wright; and their allies included writer Oscar Brown Sr., journalist Richard Durham of the *Chicago Defender* (and later, editor of *Muhammad Speaks*); Edward Dotey, founder of the Consolidated Trades Council, who ran for the state senate; and Joe Jefferson, founder of the Negro Labor Relations Board. These people were not afraid of being associated with the Communists and ignored the obvious risks of being identified as a Communist by the police, and/or blackballed by the economically powerful. There were evidently thousands more black people who admired the Communists but were afraid of making that admiration public.[33] Several family members I have interviewed echoed what June Rice, age seventy-two, said: the Communists were "troublemakers... who worked to help the community." I believe she was covering herself to determine whose side I was on. Being a Communist sympathizer is still considered a dangerous thing by the old timers.[34] Probably Horace Cayton and St. Clair Drake, authors of *Black Metropolis*, were about as accurate in their assessment of Communist popularity as anyone: "The

'Reds' won the admiration of the Negro by default. They were the only white people who seemed to really care what happened to the Negro."[35] Black people needed allies, and they were the only ones in Chicago who reached out to the black Chicagoan.

The Communists could not move the black community to embrace united action, however, because the black community had social divisions that inhibited community-wide action. Lighter-complected blacks tended to separate themselves from darker complected blacks, in churches, social organizations and political activities; preferring high church, formal social affairs and the moderate, politically, NAACP.[36] Lighter blacks often had a different historical background, being earlier refugees from the South. Often they were the sons and daughters of white men, sent North to escape the Southern "white redemption" of the 1890s, which had overturned the experiment in racial equality known as Reconstruction. The great majority of blacks in the community of the 1930s were more recent immigrants fleeing the deteriorating economy of the South. Often looked down on for their rural Southern ways, they naturally resented that condescending attitude of the light-skinned blacks.[37]

There was also a class rift within this segregated community. Forced to live together, better off, middle-class Negroes, although only about five percent of the population, nevertheless attempted to remain apart from the poor. Often, class and color seemed comparable; however, that was not the rule. Certainly, successful blacks, no matter what their shade, particularly those educated in traditionally white universities, had an attitude of putting down uneducated blacks. Similarly, dark-complected blacks who were successful held attitudes of resentment when this same attitude was applied to them also. So it happened, for example, that poor-turned-rich Jesse Binga, and Robert Abbott, founder of the *Chicago Defender*, and brilliant chemist Anthony Overton, all dark-complected, did not support the NAACP (known for its light-complected bias), nor did they attend black society's formal balls.[38]

Class distinctions came out in speech patterns, vocabulary, taste in dress, and attitude. Those distinctions were to last until the era of the late 1960s. (The Black Panther Party was involved in disrupting these distinctions and promoting racial unity behind a working-class program.)

In this social environment, a light-complected, well-educated black man, like Earl Dickerson, who empathized with the poor, was handicapped by his skin color and by his diction. Earl Dickerson was elected alderman of the Second Ward in 1939. He was remarkable in that he represented the social needs of his constituents in the city council.[39] However, it was rough, tough William Dawson, who put forth no program that addressed the major social concerns of the black community, who could appeal more to the average black voter than the intellectual Dickerson. In 1942, Dawson beat Dickerson decisively in their run for Congress.[40]

If Earl Dickerson had been so ambitious as to want a realignment of power within the city, he also would have had to reach out to the poor in other communities. Dickerson, however, was not a radical. Nevertheless, he was fired from the U.S. Fair Employment Practices Committee for his association with the Communists. Sincerity and "red" had an undeniable affinity in mid-century black Chicago. All the roughing up by police and the harassment by the federal government proved their sincerity to those who were skeptical. The average Southsider could see that a beating, or undue harassment, was a burden one did not have to take on behalf of black people. Communists took the beatings and harassment and continued to call for black/white unity. Whatever else one might say about the Communists, they appeared sincere. Of all the values their leaders had to have, the black people of Chicago put sincerity first. This statement comes from a survey by St. Clair Drake and Horace Cayton on the topic of values blacks wanted in their leaders.[41]

A factor which probably hindered the Communist cause more significantly than color and class, however, was the beleaguered existence of Depression Era Black Chicago. There was a conservatism which, although it might have appeared to be apathy, might as easily have been the community's perception of the situation it was in, and the resulting belief that the current situation was not changeable, given the circumstances. Although the black community was angry at the treatment it received, that anger came out inwardly: black-on-black violence, escapism through drugs or alcoholism, or other ways of removing oneself from reality. Psychiatrists Lionel Ovesey and A. Kardiner referred to this phenomenon as the "mark of oppression" in their 1950 book by that name. Black Americans, they offered, suffered from the psychological depression of being a powerless, violently oppressed caste.[42] When a black Chicagoan looked at his or her life, according to Drake and Cayton, it was almost as easy for him to blame the ghetto on black people as it was to blame white people. Black Chicagoans tended to blame both white racism and their own character flaws for the conditions they lived in.[43] The point being that it is doubtful anyone could have moved the black community to sustained mass action in 1930s Chicago.

By the late 1940s, the financial base for most black political independence had dissolved. The funding of black politicians through black racketeers, basically through the policy racket (the black-run lottery, illegal at that time), was lost with the takeover of that lottery by the Mafia through kidnapping, murder and political collusion.[44] Congressman Dawson's black base was swept out from under him.

Retired Judge Sydney Jones and his friend Ishmael Flory, a Communist, both were of the opinion that Dawson had wanted to help his community but was effectively silenced. They, and others, show an ambivalence toward Dawson, admiring him yet at odds with his politics. In fact, a remarkable revelation about all these politically active people is the camaraderie they felt for one another. Dawson told Communist Ray Hansboro, for example, "You handle the rabble-rousing, I'll take care of the money end of it."[45] The feelings were evidently similar between black Communist Claude Lightfoot and conservative Baptist minister Richard Kellar. On the occasion of Lightfoot's retirement, Rev. Kellar's comments were revealing: "We are waging the same warfare. If 'Top' uses socialism and I use the Bible, it's still the same struggle. We salute you 'Top'!"[46] So it was with Republican Archibald Carey and radical author Horace Cayton, who both, by the way, respected policy wheel owner Theodore Rowe, who shot it out with the Mafia.[47]

There was a spirit of forgiving and understanding based on "race" and the predicament they saw themselves all to be in. Race was an overriding consideration in mid-century black Chicago, and so was the general feeling that virtually nothing could be done about white racism or about the ghetto.[48]

That pessimistic attitude was dying, however. Congressman Dawson's career illustrates the change. Dawson, as a loyal Democrat, economically dependent on the Democratic Party, had consistently supported white Mississippians in their attempts to go slow on civil rights issues.[49] He consistently refused to support New York's black Congressman Adam Clayton Powell's anti-lynching initiative. However, in 1956, he was loudly booed by black ministers for his criticism of their growing activism.[50] The idea that poor blacks would let someone, anyone, be their figurehead leader, because we were not going any place anyway, was giving ground to the idea that the people were moving and the leaders had better catch on or move out of the way. It was this tension that was clearly, at least in part, a class tension that would forge its way to the scene. What was to come was a challenge to elite leadership, by a democratic idea that no one can lead us without our permission–because black people are going to address issues that really matter to their lives.

The decade following World War II witnessed the demise of the Communists in black Chicago. Black Communist leaders Claude Lightfoot and William Patterson were sent to jail under the Smith Act. Writer Claudia Jones and leader Benjamin Davis were deported.[51] Police brutality had done much to discourage black membership in the Communist Party, but its ties with the Union of Soviet Socialist Republics (U.S.S.R.) had done even more to disaffect the black community. The International Party had ordered the disbanding of the Communist-led unemployment councils, which had carried out the eviction resistance in the 1930s. The Hitler-Stalin Pact of 1939 did not sit well with black Communists either. Disillusioned black Communists said the Communist Party put their ideology ahead of reality. Black people were in need of housing, not ideology, they said.[52] The witch-hunting of the McCarthy Era pushed black leaders to become silent on any association with the Communist Party, and that association was largely forgotten. When the revolutionary Black Panther Party was born, its members would know none of this history, and the former Communists would have to seek them out. Even then, the Hitler-Stalin Pact would come back to haunt them.

SUMMATION

The political weakness of the Chicago ghetto was imposed by the poverty produced by racial discrimination and the effects of the Great Depression, and traditional politicians taking advantage of that poverty. Expressions of "people power" were held in check by police and Mafia violence, directed by politicians, and the threat of that violence. There were class tensions within the community, which remained secondary as long as there was little hope of meaningful change. And there was a feeling that not much could be accomplished in Chicago to better the conditions of the race. With the odds so against them, it is a wonder that some people tried radical solutions to a radically wrong situation. It was quite courageous. Still, in such an environment, radicals who did address the needs of that community were isolated from the people by police brutality and that leadership was destroyed.

The history of a radical struggle and the silencing of that struggle was not available to 1960s black youth who were about to begin their own radical struggle in Chicago in a time of rising expectations among black people. Their goal would be the same: to end racism in America. Would history repeat itself for black radical Chicagoans of the 1960s and 70s?

Notes

1. Harold F. Gosnell, *Negro Politicians* (Chicago: University of Chicago Press, 1967), 169.

2. Manning Marable, "Black Power in Chicago," *Review of Radical Political Economics* 17 (1985): 158.

3. George Robinson, "The Negro in Politics in Chicago," *Journal of Negro History* (April 1934): 220–225. See also Rayford W. Logan and Michael R. Winston, eds., *Dictionary of American Negro Biography* (New York: Norton, 1982), 362–366.

4. Horace R. Cayton and St. Clair Drake, *Black Metropolis: A Study of Negro Life in a Northern City* (New York: Harcourt, Brace, 1945), 349–351, 362–366.

5. Ibid., 488–490; Gosnell, *Negro Politicians*, 361.

6. Ibid., 622. The authors refer to these as the Negro upper class, but they are doctors, teachers, lawyers, undertakers—in short—middle-class professionals.

7. James R. Barrett, *Work and Community in the Jungle: Chicago's Packinghouse Workers, 1894–1922* (Urbana: University of Illinois Press, 1987), 215–223.

8. Ibid., 222–223.

9. William M. Tuttle Jr., *Race Riot: Chicago in the Red Summer of 1919* (New York: Atheneum, 1970), 250–251.

10. Allan H. Spear, *Black Chicago: The Making of a Negro Ghetto* (Chicago: University of Chicago Press, 1967), 221.

11. Ibid., 205–208.

12. Ibid., 41.

13. "Jesse Binga," *Journal of Negro History* (January 1973): 57–58.

14. Rita Gordon, "The Change in Political Alignment of Chicago Negroes," *Journal of American History* (December 1969): 591.

15. William Grimshaw, *Bitter Fruit: Black Politics and the Chicago Machine, 1931–1991* (Chicago: University of Chicago Press, 1992), 108–109.

16. *Chicago Daily Defender*, July 18, 1939.

17. *Fifteenth Census of the United States*; Harold F. Gosnell, *Negro Politicians* (Chicago: University of Chicago Press, 1967), 321.

18. Papers of Claude Barnett, founder and director of the Associated Negro Press, Chicago Historical Society.

19. Papers of Claude Barnett, Chicago Historical Society, Box 342, Associated Negro Press, press release, "Wave of Communism Excites Chicago's South Side."

20. *Chicago Defender*, July 8, 1939.

21. Richard C. Wade and Harold M. Mayer, *Chicago: Growth of a Metropolis*

(Chicago: University of Chicago Press, 1972), 256.

22. *Chicago Daily Defender*, August 5, 1931.

23. Interview with Sydney Jones, retired Cook County judge, Chicago, July 7, 1992. See also Barnett Papers, Chicago Historical Society, Box 342.

24. *Chicago Defender*, August 5, 1931.

25. Jones interview.

26. Barnett Papers, Chicago Historical Society. The Associated Negro Press listed the number at 15,000 "rabble"; the *Communist Daily Worker* reported 110,000; the *Chicago Tribune* estimated 25,000.

27. Horace R. Cayton and St. Clair Drake, *Black Metropolis: A Study of Negro Life in a Northern City* (New York: Harcourt, Brace, 1945), 301.

28. Gosnell, *Negro Politicians*, 336.

29. Christopher Robert Reed, "A Study of Black Politics and Protest in Depression-Decade Chicago," PhD diss., Kent State University, 1982.

30. Harry Haywood, *Black Bolshevik* (New York: International Publishers, 1979), 444.

31. Ibid., 445.

32. *Chicago Defender*, October 16, 1932.

33. Barnett Papers, Chicago Historical Society, Box 7. Communists were reportedly thousands strong in the Black community of the late 1930s according to the Associated Negro Press (ANP). See also interview with Ishmael Flory, former executive secretary of the National Negro Congress, conducted at his home, August 1993.

34. Interview with Freeman Rice and June Rice, Chicago, April 5, 1993, and with Edward Rice, Chicago, December 24, 1993.

35. St. Clair Drake and Horace R. Cayton, *Black Metropolis: A Study of Negro Life in a Northern City* (New York: Harcourt, Brace, 1945), 736.

36. Numerous references are made to this social phenomenon. See E. Franklin Frazier, *Black Bourgeoisie* (Chicago: University of Chicago Press, 1957), 103–117; Drake and Cayton, *Black Metropolis*, 494–497.

37. Frazier, *Black Bourgeoisie*, 113–115.

38. Roi Ottley, *The Lonely Warrior: The Life and Times of Robert S. Abbott* (Chicago: Henry Regnery Company, 1955), 12–23.

39. *Chicago Defender*, April 5, 1939.

40. Papers of Earl B. Dickerson, Chicago Historical Society, clippings from the April 1942 election.

41. Drake and Cayton, *Black Metropolis*, 390–395.

42. Abram Kardiner and Lionel Ovesey, *The Mark of Oppression: Explorations in the Personality of the American Negro* (Chicago: University of Chicago Press, 1951).

43. Drake and Cayton, *Black Metropolis*, 477.

44. William Grimshaw, *Bitter Fruit: Black Politics and the Chicago Machine, 1931–1991* (Chicago: University of Chicago Press, 1992), 82–84.

45. Interview with Ishmael Flory, former executive secretary of the National Negro Congress.

46. *Chicago Defender*, January 17, 1973.

47. Papers of Archibald Carey, Chicago Historical Society. See also interview with Robert Lucas, director of the Kenwood Oakland Community Organization, Chicago, August 17, 1992.

48. Drake and Cayton, *Black Metropolis*, 384–390.

49. Barnett Papers, Chicago Historical Society, Box 349, Folder 2.

50. *Chicago Tribune*, October 16, 1956.

51. Papers of Claude Lightfoot, DuSable Museum of African American History, Chicago. Interview of Claude Lightfoot conducted by Margaret Burroughs, April 18, 1970.

52. Interview with Nelson Peery, former Communist and author of *Black Fire: The Story of an American Revolutionary*, Chicago, April 13, 1994.

Chapter 2

The World of the Illinois Panthers

Social and Political Realities of Chicago's West Side in the 1960s

The Black Panther Party has been studied as a national political or social movement. The political and social conditions of Chicago, however, made for the establishment of a Black Panther movement that was uniquely Chicagoan and was relatively successful. A year after the murder of Chicago Panther leader Fred Hampton by Chicago Police officers, thousands of high school students were staging walkouts protesting his murder at over a dozen high schools.[1] This action was evidence of successful Panther cadres in most black high schools in the city. Chicago's chapter of the Black Panther Party, the Illinois Black Panther Party, was perhaps the most effective in the nation. It had as high a morale as any Panther chapter in the nation in its first two years and received some of the most devastating attention from the Federal Bureau of Investigation (FBI).

Alongside the Oakland parent chapter, the Los Angeles chapter and the New York chapter, the Chicago chapter stood out as an effectively run organization. This Chicago chapter was not a citywide success. It flourished on Chicago's black "West Side" but enjoyed less success on the black "South Side."

SOCIAL CONDITIONS

Chicago's West Side ghetto was an expanding refugee center in the 1960s. Displaced black Americans congregated there like the Palestinians did on the West Bank. Black people were coming north from Mississippi, Arkansas and Louisiana. They were being pushed off the land by mechanization, and lack of jobs, or they moved with the desire for a better life. Black Southerners came, often ejected, from their cultural base of over two hundred years, on the closest vehicle heading north, the Illinois Central Railroad.[2] They were joined there, on the West Side of Chicago, by people pushed off Chicago's South Side, where urban renewal meant removal of the poor. They came to a place where decent housing was hard to find. The communities they came to were North Lawndale, the Near West Side, East Garfield and West Garfield. Between 1950 and 1960, North Lawndale's population grew from 100,000 to 125,000 and from thirteen percent black to ninety-one percent black. Sixty-two percent of these people were from the South.[3] This means that there were some 75,000 transplanted black Southerners in North Lawndale by 1960, and more were moving in. In the 1960s, West Garfield increased in population from 45,000 to 48,000 and changed from almost all white to entirely black. It took East Garfield two decades to experience this same change between 1950 and 1970. The Near West Side's growth and racial change began in the 1940s, but was much the same.[4]

Housing on the black West Side was deteriorating and overpriced, largely due to the machinations of local realtors working to make a profit by encouraging white owners to flee and sell cheaply, then marking up the price (as much as 100 percent) for black families moving in. Real estate profits were averaging 70 percent. The people they sold the houses to often did not understand the terms of the sale, and often had to double up with other families to purchase a house.[5]

Banks refused to make loans in areas that were racially changing, so that black home buyers not only paid more for their homes, but purchased homes via contract, without equity.[6] Bank policies also meant that home improvements did not get financed in black communities.

The Federal Housing Authority, likewise, refused to advance money for rehabilitation to people moving into a racially changing neighborhood, but did advance it to those people moving out. So even federal policies encouraged white flight and discouraged community preservation.[7]

Slumlords, often absentee, raised rents and ceased to do repairs. Black families, hemmed in by segregation, paid more in home costs and in rent, due to this artificial housing scarcity created by that segregation. They were able to afford this added expense far less than whites.[8] Urban renewal on the near South Side also produced thousands of displaced poor blacks, from the area north of 35th Street and east of South Park Boulevard (now called Martin Luther King Drive). Many of these displaced South Siders went to the West Side also.[9] In the period from 1941 to 1965, Chicago displaced 160,000 poor black (and some 40,000 whites) from their homes to make way for urban renewal and expressway construction. Of these displaced people, 3,100 were provided with public housing.[10] Rigid segregation and gerrymandered school districts denied blacks open enrollment in community schools and meant the city double-shifted black schools. Decreased garbage pickup and increased population on the West Side also meant the rat population became more than the human population there.

The people of North Lawndale put up a fight to save their community, a fight that is documented by Alphine Jefferson in "Housing Discrimination and Community Response in North Lawndale (Chicago) 1948-1968." (Duke University: 1979) The dissertation tells of a creative people fighting to have a decent community. However, the pressures of banks, the federal housing authority, realtors and rent gougers, along with politicians (and add to that the high unemployment of the people on the West Side) meant that life was hard, unhealthy and often brutal.

North Lawndale, or simply Lawndale, as its residents called it, had some of the worst housing in the city by 1960; and by 1960, North Lawndale also had the highest percentage of people on welfare in the city (31 percent) and the largest average family size.[11] It had the highest crime rate in the city, and police were assigned to its Fillmore District as punishment for misconduct elsewhere.[12] However, the people were hardly complacent. The police often referred to the aggressive nature of West Side youth by referring to them as the "West Side Willies."[13]

Most of the black migrants to Chicago came with a Southern culture still very much intact. It was a culture based on the extended family.[14] Family was most important to West Siders. South side parents told their kids, "Don't talk to strangers." In contrast, a strange face on the West Side required an explanation from that person, "Who are you?"–meaning who are your cousins, aunts and uncles. If you are not related to anyone, it was implied, why are you in this neighborhood? Black West Siders hung together, conscious of a common oppressor, racist whites. Southern-born, West Side parents taught their children, "Go to school and get educated (like we could not do down south) and don't take no stuff from those white folks (like we had to down south), nor from snooty South Siders either."[15] The black people of the West Side, I am proposing, lived in a situation and had a community spirit that was ready for a revolution of some sort to occur.

Black West Siders, it was said, had a chip on their shoulders. Denigrated in Chicago public schools, where teachers, black and white, were known to say, "Why are you people so... " (loud, inattentive, ignorant, impressed with money) and abused politically, poorly housed and cheated; perhaps West Siders could be excused for developing a "chip." When a black family moved on a block, and every white family picked up their belongings and left, black people understood that, as far as Chicago was concerned, black was bad, "country" (of rural origins) was bad. Doubt crept in the psyche as to one's own worth. Being black often carried a stigma in Chicago. Underneath that doubt, however, was a toughness and an acknowledgment of that toughness. There was a pride in that toughness–not a pride necessarily in being black, which is an accident of birth–but in being able to take what white racist Chicago dished out. This is my opinion of West Siders after living and working among them for four years (1970-1974).

Black gangs formed on the West Side to fight off the white gangs that, at first, ran them home, often with police help. The Egyptian Cobras, the Vice Lords, the Clovers and the Navajos were known all over the city for their fighting abilities. They were less willing to defer to the police, which the toughest South Side gangs did almost automatically. And as far as they were concerned, the police were the largest, best-armed gang.[16]

Where the bad feelings began, between the Chicago police and the black community, is probably in racial politics coupled with the ethnocentrism of the average police officer. Documented cases of police abuses were common in the Chicago Defender in the 1950s and through the 1960s. Abusive language, arbitrary arrests, and searches without provocation, torturing of arrestees, refusal to assist people in distress, and laxness in arresting certain criminals were the most common complaints. These complaints were met consistently with denials of any wrongdoing by police and elected officials.[17]

An interesting development of the late 1960s was to watch how urbanized black youth on the South Side responded to violent police versus how black youth responded on the West Side.

Aldermen stuck by police, and the police stuck together. Chicago politicians had a lot of influence on the Chicago Police Department. Becoming a police officer usually required the approval of the local ward committeeman (who was usually the alderman), and the job-holder was, therefore, often beholden to that ward officer. In Chicago, in the 1960s, the key positions in the police department were thus controlled by the local Democratic Party.[18] Thousands of police probably did a creditable job; nevertheless, the politicians used favoritism to advance officers most pliable to the Democratic machine and beholden to other, less ethical interests. The case of Officer Richard Cain, a mob-controlled "satchel man" in the police department, is instructive. Cain's influential friends worked wonders for his career before he was caught. Politicians used favoritism to advance officers most pliable to the Democratic machine or to other interests. In that sense, the police department was an arm of the Cook County Democratic Party. From the black West Sider's perspective, the white Democrats ruled, and the police (actually certain police) were their military.[19]

West Siders were not only oppressed by the worst policing, but were segregated from black South Siders, according to Alphine Jefferson, through screening renters and high rents.[20] Black South Siders, urbanized and more of an individualistic mindset, represented successful, ambitious individuals. The problem was that black Chicagoans, even on the South Side, did not have enough success to go around. That scarcity of possibilities split up families as well as the community. So a minority of the black South Siders had moved to the Southern extremity of that ghetto—the Chatham neighborhood and scratched out some financial success, largely by servicing the black poor as their school teachers, funeral directors, barbers, and postmen. The South Side, in fact, had a range of incomes much broader than that on the West Side. In fact, the most intense poverty in Chicago was in the near South Side.[21] South Siders lacked the community spirit of West Siders. Instead, they had a class rift, and some of them enjoyed the benefits of political power in ways in which no black West Sider did.

Chicago's newest, most powerless ghetto, the West Side, was not troubled with class antagonisms, nor was it as knowledgeable about the city. It certainly had a spirit that the South Side lacked in the 1960s. Where book knowledge was lacking, gut knowledge was strong and perceptive. West Siders often responded from their intuition and acted rather than discussed. As a result, the West Side had a reputation as tough and aggressive.

There are numerous examples of West Side militancy vs. South Side complacency. In the period 1965-1968, there were three major black riots in Chicago. All three of these riots occurred exclusively on the West Side. The armed Deacons for Defense (also chartered with the NRA as the National Negro Rifle Association) was a West Side phenomenon. They armed themselves to protect black citizens primarily from racist and violent police.[22] There was no comparable organization on the South Side. The Contract Buyers League split into West Side and South Side factions over the South Siders' perception of West Siders as too militant.[23]

TRADITIONAL WEST SIDE POLITICS

Since the days of slain, black ward committeeman candidate Octavius Granady in the "bloody 20th" Ward (now part of the 1st and 27th wards),[24] West Side politics has been more violent than North or South Side politics.[25] The 20th Ward gets its "bloody" nickname from the list of political people assassinated there. In the years 1926-1930, four black men involved in politics were murdered in the 20th Ward. The Granady murder set the political tone for West Side politics for the next fifty years, so it is instructive. Granady, a well-known black lawyer, was running for ward committeeman on April 10, 1928, election day, when he was gunned down, in broad daylight, by five uniformed police officers, with the assistance of a second car full of Italian gangsters, in front of several eyewitnesses. The police who investigated Granady's murder were the same police who had done the deed, according to eyewitnesses. One of these eyewitnesses was murdered, and the jury was threatened, and the prosecutor of the police had his office burglarized.[26] Despite damning testimony, the judge was so hostile that the special Assistant District Attorney Frank Loesch quit his prosecution, and the case was declared nolle pross.[27] Loesch later boasted of the effect his prosecution had on the Eller hoodlums (Eller was the 20th Ward Committeeman). Granady's murder epitomized West Side politics, illustrating how far politicians were willing to go to keep blacks under their control, and how boldly they operated when killing black men in politics. It was still a common subject of conversation in 1963 when black alderman Ben Lewis was killed.[28]

The vote on the 1960s West Side was relatively meaningless, tied, as it was, to a Democratic precinct captain's favors. The local Democratic

Party's backbone was its precinct captains. They dispensed favors to needy people and punished those who did not go along with politics as usual.[29]

Failure to vote Democratic could cost a citizen a job, rejection of a needed license, intense inspection by city building inspectors, etc. West Side precinct captains knew how a citizen voted because they generally accompanied voters into the voting booth.[30]

The Democratic political machine in the early 1960s ruled the West Side with an iron hand by punishment and by favors, and was inclined to use violence to keep black people away from independent politics. For example, Edward "Gus" Savage, who ran the community newspaper called the *Westside Booster*, was threatened and boycotted, and his store windows stoned until he was forced to take his independent newspaper to the South Side and rename it the *Chatham Citizen*. On the South Side, the paper flourished, and Savage eventually became a U.S. Congressman.[31] Political independent Richard Barnett related how his tires were slashed and windows broken around every election day. He began to buy old tires for the month before the election. Likewise, independent alderman Danny Davis remembered having to carry a pistol and having had numerous fights with bottles, bricks and bats with Ed Quigley's boys.[32] Neither Danny Davis nor any other independent was successful in the decade of the 1960s, the decade in which the members of the Illinois Black Panther Party came of voting age.[33]

West Side politics was called "plantation politics" in reference to plantation slavery in the old South, and these West Side wards were known as the "plantation wards," controlled by the politician/mob brotherhood Frank Loesch had fought forty years earlier. Black independent Bernetta Howell ran for Congress in 1964 against the regular Democrat, Irish, Thomas J. O'Brien. O'Brien died two weeks before the election and still won by a landslide.[34] As historian Alphine Jefferson argues, "If there ever was a colonial set-up, the West Side was it. Men work for the city...if they don't do as they're told, they lose their jobs."[35]

West Side black political activists began the push to take control of their communities in the late 1950s and early 1960s. They began by forming local organizations, like the Garfield Organization, which ran Curtis Foster for alderman of the 29th ward in 1963. Local white aldermen were well-entrenched, however, and known as the West Side bloc. They were a cadre of white politicians and gangsters who ran the 24th, 25th, 27th, 29th and 28th Wards.[36] Although all five wards were majority black, "Izzy" Horowitz, Jewish, ran the 24th; Italian Vito

Marzullo ran the 25th; Irishman Edward Quigley ran the 27th; Bernie Neinstein (Jewish) ran the 29th, and Italian Joseph Jambrone ran the 28th.[37] Racism filtered down through the ranks. Of some 63 precincts in the all-black 24th Ward, in 1960, 59 had white precinct captains.[38] The West Side bloc politicians could not keep these black people unrepresented for long, however, and they knew it. They needed to select successors who would follow orders. "The last thing I need," said Bernie Neinstein, "is a smart nigger."[39] They picked Ben Lewis to run the 24th Ward. Lewis, a black man, was fronted by the local Jews. He spoke Yiddish and called Bernie Neinstein "Mr. Neinstein." Neinstein called him "Ben."[40] On the surface, Lewis appeared to be a pliant tool, but he did things for his community that evidenced an independent mind. Political activist Richard Barnett is convinced that Lewis's apparent "Uncle Tomism" was a ruse. It was Lewis, he says, who prevented high-rise housing projects in the ward, insisted on garbage collections twice a week and fought the idea of double-shifted schools.[41]

Lewis also challenged the Elrod insurance business, run by former ward committeeman Arthur Elrod's family, which had a monopoly on insurance in that ward—until Ben Lewis set up his own insurance business there. The politics of this money-making venture are illustrative of the "corruption-is-normal" mindset of Chicago in the 1960s. Part of Chicago politics was the ward committeeman's control of liquor licenses. Since liquor store owners needed a license, the committeeman usually created an insurance company to pressure the store owner to buy the committeeman's insurance in exchange for his license.[42] Arthur Elrod, the previous committeeman, had an insurance monopoly on this practice in Lewis's ward.[43]

There were rumors that Alderman Ben Lewis was even considering setting up a bank to compete with the white monopoly on this in his ward. All in all, Ben Lewis made a number of moves that did not go along with the West Side bloc.

On February 27, 1963, the West Side's first black alderman, Ben Lewis, was shot execution style (three 32 caliber bullets in the back of his head), while he was handcuffed on the floor. He had not put up a struggle, according to newspaper reports. Republican alderman John Hoellen identified the likely culprits as the police/politicians linkage of the West Side bloc, and called for an investigation.[44] Not a single black alderman (and there were six, all South Siders) opened his mouth in support of the investigation white Republican Hoellen called for. The

22

city's daily newspapers alluded to Lewis's love affairs and his gambling, but when the police investigator found clues that some police officers might have been involved, the editors dropped the story, and the investigator was removed from the case.[45] The incident looked suspiciously like the Granady murder of thirty-five years earlier, and to anyone looking in from the outside, the media and black politicians looked like accomplices.

Whether the West Side bloc had Ben Lewis killed or not will probably never be known. The perception among black activists in his community is that Lewis's independence got him killed.[46]

That Lewis's death was *perceived* as an assassination, and due to his commitment to his community rather than to the Democratic Party, is most fundamental. It is out of such perceptions that carrying weapons, and independent politics, and even revolution are legitimized.

Previously, blacks had been killed by the political/police/mob triumvirate, and as far as West Side activists were concerned, this murder was more of that same phenomenon. In response, several of them formed the Friends of Ben Lewis, an armed guard which accompanied black independent political speakers on the West Side.[47]

West Side Grassroots Politics

Although active and aggressive West Siders were locked out of the traditional political process, it did not mean they were politically inactive. The West Side bloc's violent handling of independent-thinking blacks simultaneously intimidated some West Siders *and* created a maverick movement of considerable strength.

Edward "Fats" Crawford was not intimidated by the Lewis murder or other tactics the West Side bloc used, like bricked windows, death threats, or police harassment. He, Ernest Thomas and scores of friends formed the Friends of Ben Lewis after Lewis's murder, which provided armed guards for black activists. In 1965, they re-named themselves the Deacons for Defense and Justice and took out a charter with the National Rifle Association, arming themselves with M-1 rifles.[48] Crawford asserted that there were over 200 Deacons on the West Side, allied with local youth clubs. Regardless of their numbers, they were a force that commanded respect on the West Side, largely, the local activists say, because they stood up to the police.[49] The Deacons also monitored the actions of the police and threatened the local store owners they felt discriminated against black people. They sent food to civil rights marchers in the South and counseled young black men. They even attended a Nazi rally in all-white Gage Park, to keep surveillance on the Nazis.[50]

The Chicago Police Department's Surveillance Unit, known as the "Red Squad," labeled the Deacon's leader, Crawford, "a known associate of everything dirty in Lawndale"[51] and evidently shot up their office on October 2, 1966.[52]

Frederick "Doug" Andrews, founder of the Garfield Organization, and Russ Meeks, founder of Search for Truth, were, like Crawford, committed to political action on behalf of the West Side black community. Doug Andrews was perhaps the most popular of the West Side activists. According to Judge Eugene Pincham, who later defended Andrews, in 1970, on an arson and rioting charge, Doug Andrews could have been elected mayor of the West Side, had there been such an office. Other activists, Richard Barnett, Bernetta Barrett and Danny Davis, agree.[53] Andrews was guilty in fact of both arson and rioting, caught in the act of firebombing by a photographer. However, there was an old mountain man on the jury, an old Southerner from the hills, who understood what black West Siders understood: if the government does not treat you fairly, you have no obligation to treat the government fairly. And so, Doug Andrews went free with the jury hung.[54]

In 1968, Doug Andrews led a "boycott the polls" campaign, which cost the Democratic Party at least 30,000 votes, and then parlayed with President Nixon to get financing for his Garfield Organization. Andrews, it is said, was rewarded with control over Burger King franchises on the West Side.[55] Edward Crawford, Doug Andrews and hundreds of their friends and followers in the Deacons and the Garfield Organization, as well as those in Russ Meeks's group and in the gangs (the Vice Lords and the Cobras), were a force for change pushed outside traditional politics by the machine. Chicago politics worked so well at excluding them that the more spirited of them worked not to get into that system, but to overthrow it. Many of them would join the Illinois Black Panther Party.

The Chicago Freedom Movement

July 10, 1966, is remembered as an extremely hot day. It was the day of the giant rally at Soldier Field in Chicago, where approximately 60,000 people turned out to listen to Dr. Martin Luther King Jr.[56] Black political activists from Chicago had gone south to help civil rights efforts in the south, and the wall of race segregation had come down. Jim Crow segregation had seemed an unchanging fact of Southern life, yet in a decade of struggle, it had come apart. Almost miraculously, it had been taken apart by a people who had nothing but courage and commitment to a cause. In this victory over impossible odds was the promise of even greater accomplishments, as many activists saw it.[57] There was an air of hope present. This was racist, segregated Chicago, with its history of overcrowded black neighborhoods and under financed schools. Dr. King had come north to participate in the desegregation of Chicago from de facto, as opposed to de jure, segregation (segregation by law), as it was called.

The Andrew McPherson Quartet was playing "John Brown's Body" when more than fifty teenagers burst onto the playing field of the stadium, with a large, red flag. They were shouting something. Probably, they shouted "Mighty Blackstone!" or "Stone Love!" for these teenagers represented the largest gang in Chicago at that time, the Blackstone Rangers. They interrupted the quartet, stopped Dr. King from coming out, and upset all the "muckety-mucks" (colloquial for people who think themselves important) as they circled the field on the run. The poor boys had begun to enter the civil rights movement in Chicago. The crowd of largely middle-class people did not like it. They thought, "Can't anyone do something to stop them?–stop these rough boys from Woodlawn." Disc jockey Herb Kent tried, but they ignored him. Kent did not speak their language. He was an "Ivy Leaguer" (assimilationist), and they were "gouster" (boys from the rough 'hood'). Entertainer Dick Gregory tried also, and they understood him, but this was their thing right now. They wanted to be a part of the civil rights movement as a power.[58] They, as political representatives of poor black youth, were in their own way asking the people of the mainstream, "Does this new inclusion of non-white Americans in society include us?"[59]

Meanwhile, the crowd seemed to get angry. "Call the police!" many people yelled, and more people cheered that idea.[60] A large part of the crowd thought the police were on *their* side. However, the police never came, and the gang, or club, eventually charged into the upper east side of the stadium and let the rally continue. This was the beginning of the Chicago Freedom Movement (CFM).

The CFM was morally inspired, pushing for assimilation. It was law-abiding, except where the law transgressed "right" and "wrong." At that point, it sanctioned civil disobedience. And that was the point at which it would clash with the city police, who tended to be both arrogant and racially biased. Generally speaking, police had no sympathy with the civil rights movement and tended to see disorder, whether caused by demonstrators or gangsters, as criminal.[61]

"Respectable Negroes" in Chicago had, for decades, tried to distance themselves from the poorer, rougher black people and prove their worthiness to "white" America. The police attitude, however, that blacks, generally speaking, were criminals, pushed along a transformation in the wind that was saying to the youth of the "respectables," "We have nothing to prove! We are who we are, black people! Love the people!" The experiences of the CFM over the next two years worked that transformation for the youthful activists, and they became rebels against the hypocrisy of "respectability." Further on, I will show how that transformation took place.

The community leaders who organized the Chicago Freedom Movement—which began with that giant rally, and the posting of fifty demands on the door at City Hall, July 1 0, 1966—had a fairly good idea of what created the conditions of a black ghetto. The evidence is right there in those fifty demands. They were directed at real estate brokers, banks, the federal housing authority, the Democratic Party, the Chicago Board of Education, and the local trade unions.[62] They indicated that the profit from the dual housing market, bolstered by the policies of banks, the federal housing authority, and the local political machine, and the manipulation of the prejudices of white homeowners, all worked in symbiosis to produce the conditions of the ghetto.[63] Racist politics also produced a segregated, unequal school system. The factors that tied these interests were economic profit for most and political control of the poor for the political machine.[64] The consequences were an unhealthy living environment for the poor and an immense waste of lives and of money for our society as a whole.[65] That day of the rally, Dr. King let it be known where he stood when he said:

> We will be sadly mistaken if we think freedom is some lavish dish
> that the federal government will pass out on a silver platter… This
> day we must decide to fill up the jails of Chicago if necessary in
> order to end slums…We must make it clear that we will purge
> Chicago of every politician, whether he be Negro or white
> [emphasis mine] who feels that he owns the Negro vote.[66]

Dr. King understood that in Chicago, the law did not confine his movement, and race did not necessarily define the oppressor.

The Chicago Freedom Movement was a coalition of civil rights-oriented community groups that had worked together to desegregate Chicago public schools and had failed. They had involved the children in a school boycott that had successfully resisted elected black politicians in 1963 and again in 1964, but had not succeeded at much else. Here was a piece of information that would begin to transform the movement. The first-line enemies of reform, or revolutionary changes in the black ghetto, were the black people elected to represent that community. Furthermore, this failure had weakened the hold of its activist leaders on their youthful followers. Failure will do that to a reform movement. Young people, motivated by Al Raby through the Student Woodlawn Area Project, became skeptics of the non-violent civil disobedience tactics because they had not worked, yet, and that meant they were more open to hear a different message, if one came along.[67]

A West Side summit, the previous year, between Mayor Daley and several West Side community leaders had likewise failed to produce action on any of these grievances which the West Siders desired: 1) resignation of precinct captains who did not live in the community, 2) a civilian review board on police brutality, 3) a local voice in federally-funded programs, 4) equal job opportunities in city jobs, 5) city influence over bank loan policies, and 6) community influence in community schools. These were the heartfelt grievances of those black West Side communities, and the youth were watching to see how effective their adult leaders would be. Mayor Daley ignored ALL the demands–except to lecture West Side leaders on the suggestion that Chicago Police needed a review board.[68]

Among the groups involved with the school boycott and the CFM was the Chicago Student Non-violent Coordinating Committee (SNCC) organization, including Monroe Sharp, Bobby Rush, and Bob Brown.[69] Both South Siders, Bobby Rush and Bob Brown, a few years later, were instrumental in forming the Illinois Chapter of the Black Panther Party. And among the followers of the West Side community leaders who were rebuffed by Mayor Daley were Jewel Cook and Billy Lamar Brooks, both later founding members of that same revolutionary organization. The difference between them was that in the 1960s, all the black West Side had, politically speaking, were maverick organizations.

Perhaps that was not necessarily a negative thing because, on the South Side, the black elected officials could use money, political organization, thugs, misleading stories in the major newspapers, and, in short, all the power of the city politics to stop their fellow blacks. On the black South Side was an air of distrust, looking over one's shoulder at your "brothers," that was not present on the black West Side.

In 1966, however, the activists in the movement, black and white, got assistance from the Southern Christian Leadership Conference (SCLC) and Dr. King–whom Chicago's black South Side Congressman William Dawson labeled an unwanted "outside agitator." "Desegregation isn't needed here," Congressman Dawson said. The Chicago NAACP echoed Dawson; King, they said, was "intemperate."[70]

Dr. King came to Chicago that summer (1966) and led the march from the Soldier Field rally to City Hall, posting the CFM's fifty demands. Following that big march, the CFM's first pragmatic action was a non-violent protest march on realtors in the all-white Gage Park community, where they had previously sent testing home buyers, some black and some white, to see if both races would be shown the same list of available homes. They were not.[71]

The goal of the CFM was to free Chicago of de facto segregation. The means was non-violent civil disobedience. The CFM attracted the young, idealistic college-educated people, black and white, who had been witnessing the desegregation of the South, first-hand or on television. These people included David Finke, of the American Friends, and Patricia Berg, of the Student Woodlawn Area Project. They believed, at the time, that they could attack prejudice with love, and segregationists could be won over through the courage of non-violence.[72] They were committed to erasing the problems of the black ghetto by erasing the ghetto. They were marching for open housing in Chicago as a step in the process of creating a color blind society.

However, the older, more politically sophisticated activists, like Bob Lucas of the Congress on Racial Equality (CORE), felt they knew better. Lucas believed the more presence of open-housing marchers in these segregated white communities would provoke a violent response and embarrass the local Democratic Party with their vividly displayed racism. He hoped that the Cook County Democratic Party would be forced to the bargaining table to preserve the tenuous alliance that the Party in fact was (that Party being an alliance of white segregationists and black people, most of whom longed for the end of ghettoization). Lucas risked his safety for his community, knowing the risk involved, and went along with non-violence, as a tactic, as long as it worked.[73]

The mood among youth on the West Side of Chicago was more in tune with Bob Lucas than with the young idealists like Pat Burg and

David Finke. West Side youth were already skeptical of King's non-violent tactics.[74] In fact, the youth of the West Side community had apparently reached the threshold of what they were willing to put up with. The riot that broke out on July 12, 1966, was ostensibly the result of a hassle between police and black teens over a fire hydrant. The teens opened the hydrant to give relief to toddlers in the stifling heat, who had no swimming pool available because three of the four pools in the immediate vicinity were not open to blacks.[75] By clubbing five youths bloody, the police aggravated the tension in the community. The next day, when a police official lectured the youth on their unlawful behavior (opening the hydrant), the neighborhood of East Garfield erupted in fire bombings of white-owned stores and rock throwing at police cars. The police were unable to contain the violence, and the National Guard was called in. Once calm was established, twenty-four hours later, the police re-entered the neighborhood, and a few of them shot up several homes in retaliation.[76] "We could have stopped this rioting the first day by laying out two of those guys with [our] guns," a police officer related.[77] His answer to social problems rested in his holster.

The riot not only gave ample indication that Dr. King's non-violent approach was being met with skepticism in black Chicago, but also gave white residents of Gage Park reason to be apprehensive about black people marching on their community. This was particularly true because the news media portrayed the riot as irrational violence, thus bolstering that image of blacks as a violent, criminal people.[78]

Just two weeks later, on July 30, 1966, over three hundred fifty open-housing marchers assembled at New Friendship Baptist Church. The groups included blacks, whites, priests, nuns, ministers and Blackstone Rangers (who served as parade marshals and were sworn to non-violence). They were led by Dr. King and two flag bearers, one carrying the American flag and the other a brown flag with an "End the Slums" motto.[79] They marched into Gage Park through a mob of angry whites, yelling jeers and insults at them. The crowd of whites seemed to feel the safety of their neighborhood was at stake. They had struggled hard to preserve their community and seemed to regard open housing as a carrier of crime, bad housing, and lower property values.[80] They attacked the marchers with bricks, bottles and firecrackers. They were just warming up. Discovering some of the cars the marchers had used to get to Gage Park, they turned them over, split open the gas tanks and tossed in lighted matches. Amidst the dull booms of exploding gasoline, heard blocks away, the marchers found their police protection suddenly melting away, and then the full unhindered fury of the mob was upon them.[81]

For these open-housing marchers, the Blackstone Rangers became their heroes, leaping into the air to catch rocks, bottles and bricks, with baseball gloves.[82] Meanwhile, community leader "Ma" Houston prayed loudly and effectively, "Oh Lord, you see that boy in the plaid shirt with the brick? Tell him to put that brick down, Lord!" You see that man with the cherry bomb? Tell him not to throw it, Lord!"[83]

Once back in the Englewood community, the marchers assembled again, carrying many wounded and some unconscious persons. The floor of the church was red with blood.[84] The racist town of Cicero, just west of Chicago, was to be next.

Meanwhile, back on the South Side, Alderman Claude Holman was doggedly trying to disrupt the movement. He sent his thugs, including 300-pound "Tiny" Wilson, to take the names of the neighborhood people who attended CFM rallies.[85] The young activists were getting a course in "democratic" Chicago politics.

Before the march into Cicero could take place, Daley and four CFM leaders, including Dr. King, held a summit. The marches had become the national embarrassment that marchers had hoped they'd be to the local Democratic Party, and a threat to Daley's hold on the black community. Daley put forth an agreement that vaguely promised to end segregation and improve housing in Chicago, but offered no means of enforcing its goals. Instead of taking the offer back to the CFM rank and file, the four leaders agreed to it—without consulting fellow leaders. The leaders of CORE, SNCC and the West Side Organization were antagonized. Many of their youthful followers felt betrayed.[86]

King himself later admitted that this decision was a serious error.[87] Hindsight also shows clearly that the agreement was meaningless. The only behavior it changed was that of the marchers. They stopped demonstrating and gave up the only weapon blacks had to ameliorate the conditions of the ghetto.[88]

The West Side Organization, SNCC and CORE repudiated the agreement and called for the march into Cicero.[89] And these marchers were not dedicated to non-violence. Those that marched on September 7, 1966, just weeks after black teen Jerome Huey had been beaten to death by white teens for job hunting in Cicero, traded jeers, catcalls and bricks with the crowd of hecklers. There were about 290 marchers, and almost all were black. There were several hundred hecklers, and the Illinois

National Guard was present. In spite of the National Guard, the two crowds managed to have a big fight at the end of the march. Non-violent civil disobedience was about dead in Chicago as a tactic. As August Meier and Leon Rudwick would note in their history of CORE, "courageous, persistent non-violence produced puny gradualism, laws grudgingly written and half-heartedly enforced."[90] And for the young people who had participated in the Chicago Freedom Movement, the violence that they had faced was an awakening to the intensity of Chicago's racism. Integration as an immediate goal probably made little sense against that kind of determination. As for non-violence as a tactic, it made less sense in Chicago than it did in the South. Dr. King's philosophy had less appeal than Malcolm X's political philosophy. Malcolm said the things that appealed to urban black youth. The ghetto hustler, he had said, has less respect for the establishment's power structure than anyone else (recruit him)... don't try to integrate with the white man, he doesn't want to integrate with you. Take over your own community so that when you go to the white man, you get respect from mutual strength.[91] And then these youthful activists began to read Frantz Fanon:

> The European elite undertook to manufacture a native elite. They picked out promising adolescents; they branded them…with the principles of Western culture; they stuffed their mouths full with high-sounding phrases, grand glutinous words that stuck to the teeth. They were sent home, whitewashed. These walking lies had nothing left to say to their brothers…A new generation came on the scene…saying…there is one duty to be done, one end to achieve; to thrust out colonialism by every means.[92]

This was the core of belief out of which the Black Panther Party would grow, in the writings of Malcolm X and Fanon. Black youth had become distrustful of a moderate leadership that had accomplished nothing and felt colonialism described their situation. They would go where the writings of Malcolm X led them.

Notes

1. *Chicago Sun-Times*, December 5, 1970.

2. Arnold R. Hirsch, *Making the Second Ghetto: Race and Housing in Chicago, 1940–1960* (Cambridge: Cambridge University Press, 1983), 2, 5, 17. See also Evelyn M. Kitagawa and Karl E. Taeuber, eds., *Local Community Fact Book for the Chicago Metropolitan Area, 1980* (Chicago: Chicago Community Inventory, University of Chicago, 1983), 79, 82.

3. Alphine Jefferson, "Housing Discrimination and Community Response in North Lawndale (Chicago), Illinois, 1948–1968," PhD diss., Duke University, 1979, 66–67.

4. Kitagawa and Taeuber, *Local Community Fact Book*, 70, 74, 79, 82.

5. Jefferson, "Housing Discrimination and Community Response in North Lawndale," 70–89; Hirsch, *Making the Second Ghetto*, 29.

6. Jefferson, "Housing Discrimination and Community Response in North Lawndale," 80–84; Hirsch, *Making the Second Ghetto*, 33.

7. Hirsch, *Making the Second Ghetto*, 10–13; Jefferson, "Housing Discrimination and Community Response in North Lawndale," 170–204.

8. Jefferson, "Housing Discrimination and Community Response in North Lawndale," 72.

9. Jefferson, "Housing Discrimination and Community Response in North Lawndale," 72–74.

10. Peter Knauss, *Chicago: A One-Party State* (Chicago: University of Illinois Press, 1974), 20.

11. Jefferson, "Housing Discrimination and Community Response in North Lawndale," 12–19.

12. Interview with Leroy Martin, former superintendent, Chicago Police Department, December 24, 1994; and interview with Richard Brzeczek, former superintendent, Chicago Police Department, April 1996. This statement was originally made to the author by police officer Howard Saffold in August 1982. Both retired superintendents corroborated it.

13. Interview with Howard Saffold, Afro-American Patrolmen's League, August 1982.

14. Interviews conducted by the author with Black West Side residents reflecting these values. Especially helpful were interviews with Floyd Thomas, Harry Reese, Joe Shaw, and Anthony Jackson, November 20, 1994; interviews with Jewel Cook and Cleveland Cook in the fall of 1983; and several interviews with Billy Brooks. The author also draws on personal experiences and conversations with friends, in-laws, and neighbors.

15. Same interviews as above.

16. Interviews with three former gang members who wished to remain

anonymous.

17. *Chicago Daily Defender*, March 5–13, 1958, a series of articles on police brutality in the Black community.

18. William F. Roemer Jr., *Man Against the Mob* (New York: Ivy Books, 1989), 211.

19. Corroborated by interviews with Edward "Fats" Crawford, April 1982; Richard Barnett, August 1989; Illa Daggert, January 1981; Bernetta Howell Barrett, April 1994; and Gale Cincotta, July 1995.

20. Jefferson, "Housing Discrimination and Community Response in North Lawndale," 73.

21. *Census of Population and Housing: Nineteenth Census of the United States* (Washington, DC: U.S. Government Printing Office), census tracts, Chicago SMSA.

22. Interview with Edward "Fats" Crawford, July 1982. Crawford, one of the founders of the Deacons for Defense, explained the origins of the organization. His account was corroborated in interviews with political activist Richard Barnett; Congressman Danny K. Davis; aldermanic candidate Floyd Thomas; and 29th Ward precinct captain Harry Reese.

23. Jefferson, "Housing Discrimination and Community Response in North Lawndale," 220–233.

24. David Fremon, *Chicago Politics, Ward by Ward* (Bloomington: Indiana University Press, 1988), 179–180.

25. Fremon, *Chicago Politics*, 179.

26. Papers of Claude Barnett and the Associated Negro Press, Chicago Historical Society, Box 349, Folder 8, "Granady."

27. *Chicago Tribune*, November 28–29, 1929.

28. All of the Black politically independent activists interviewed by the author were aware of the Granady murder, although it had occurred more than fifty years earlier.

29. Grimshaw, *Bitter Fruit*, 120; Peter Knauss, *Chicago: A One-Party State*, 11.

30. "Democratic Voting—West Side Style," *Chicago Sun-Times*, November 11, 1968.

31. Interview with Eugene Pincham, judge and founder of the Harold Washington Party, August 19, 1993. This interview corroborated an earlier interview with Black political activist Bennett Johnson, July 1990.

32. Quigley was ward committeeman, or ward "boss," of the 27th Ward on Chicago's West Side.

33. Interviews with Danny K. Davis, Richard Barnett, Bernetta Howell Barrett, Illa Daggert, and Harry Reese.

34. Interview with Bernetta Howell Barrett, Chicago, March 17, 1997.

35. Jefferson, "Housing Discrimination and Community Response in North

Lawndale," 67. This sentiment was echoed by activist Richard Barnett as well as Bernetta Howell Barrett and Danny K. Davis.

36. Fremon, *Chicago Politics, Ward by Ward*, 179–181.

37. Barnett interview. See also Grimshaw, *Bitter Fruit*, 119–121.

38. Barnett interview.

39. Barnett interview.

40. Barnett interview.

41. Barnett interview.

42. Thomas Millea, *Ghetto Fever* (Milwaukee: Bruce Publishing Company, 1968), 95–96. This account was also echoed by Richard Barnett.

43. Interview with Congressman Danny K. Davis, April 1994.

44. *Muhammad Speaks*, April 1, 1963.

45. *Chicago Sun-Times*, March 4, 1963.

46. Interviews with Richard Barnett, Bernetta Howell Barrett, Floyd Thomas, and Harry Reese all support this interpretation. South Side community activist Robert Lucas, president of the Kenwood–Oakland Community Organization, also concurred in an interview conducted in August 1993.

47. Interview with Floyd Thomas, former president of the Chicago chapter of the Deacons for Defense and Justice, November 20, 1994. This interview corroborated an earlier interview with Edward "Fats" Crawford, who was reportedly beaten to death by police on October 17, 1983.

48. Papers of the Chicago Police Department, Intelligence Division, Chicago Historical Society. Files on the Deacons for Defense were among several police surveillance files turned over to the Chicago Historical Society as a result of litigation against the City of Chicago regarding illegal surveillance activities by the Chicago Police Department. A report from 1964 records that Edward Crawford purchased 200 M-1 rifles at a suburban gun store and paid in cash.

49. Interview with Harry Reese, Anthony Jackson, and Floyd Thomas, Chicago, November 20, 1994.

50. Reese and Thomas interview, November 20, 1994; see also earlier interview with Edward Crawford, 1981.

51. Papers of the Chicago Police Surveillance Unit (commonly known as the "Red Squad Papers"), Chicago Historical Society, folder marked "Deacons."

52. Interview with Edward Crawford. The account was also supported by former Deacon Floyd Thomas. Members of the Deacons asserted that police shot up their office. While no independent source has corroborated this claim, the allegation is consistent with the political climate of the time, including reports that Ku Klux Klan members served in the Fillmore District police station and that similar activities were attributed to police on the West Side by multiple sources.

53. Interviews with Eugene Pincham (August 1993), Bernetta Howell Barrett, Richard Barnett, and Danny K. Davis.

54. Pincham interview.

55. Lucy Montgomery Papers, DuSable Museum of African American History, Chicago. A document in the collection claims that the "Boycott the Polls" campaign led by Doug Andrews cost the Democratic Party 320,000 votes. However, voting statistics for West Side bloc wards show a decrease of approximately 30,000 votes in the presidential election year 1968 compared with the previous election year, 1966. See *A Handbook of Contemporary American Voting Statistics* (Pittsburgh: Governmental Affairs Institute, 1968).

56. Interview with Phil Cohran, August 1982.

57. Interview with political activist Bennett Johnson, founder of the League of Negro Voters, and Herman Gilbert, activist and author of *The Negotiations*, July 11, 1992.

58. Cohran interview.

59. Rev. John Fry, *Locked Out Americans: A Memoir* (New York: Harper & Row, 1973), 51.

60. Personal remembrance of the author.

61. Jerome H. Skolnick, *The Politics of Protest* (New York: Simon & Schuster, 1969), 263–266.

62. Alan B. Anderson and George W. Pickering, *Confronting the Color Line: The Broken Promise of the Civil Rights Movement in Chicago* (Athens: University of Georgia Press, 1986), 208–209.

63. Hirsch, *Making the Second Ghetto*, 257–259, 263–275.

64. Grimshaw, *Bitter Fruit*, 96–97; Hirsch, *Making the Second Ghetto*, 129, 274–275.

65. Jefferson, "Housing Discrimination and Community Response in North Lawndale," 250–258.

66. Manning Marable, "Black Power in Chicago," *Review of Radical Political Economics* 17 (1985): 171.

67. Millea, *Ghetto Fever*, 24.

68. Anderson and Pickering, *Confronting the Color Line*, 210.

69. Interview with Patrice Roselle (formerly Patricia Berg), former president of Chicago SNCC, June 3, 1994.

70. Marable, "Black Power in Chicago," 165, 173.

71. Anderson and Pickering, *Confronting the Color Line*, 210–212.

72. Interview with David Finke, April 11, 1984; interview with Patricia Berg, August 14, 1994.

73. Interview with Robert Lucas, president of the Kenwood Oakland Community Organization (KOCO) and former president of CORE, August

15, 1992.

74. Anderson and Pickering, *Confronting the Color Line*, 209.

75. Millea, *Ghetto Fever*, 38–39.

76. Millea, *Ghetto Fever*, 39–42.

77. Anderson and Pickering, *Confronting the Color Line*, 213.

78. Anderson and Pickering, *Confronting the Color Line*, 214–215.

79. Anderson and Pickering, *Confronting the Color Line*, 226–229.

80. Hirsch, *Making the Second Ghetto*, 35–36.

81. Finke interview.

82. Finke interview.

83. Finke interview.

84. Finke interview.

85. Finke interview. Robert Lucas also agreed that Alderman Holman was among the most vocal critics of the Chicago Freedom Movement and reportedly threatened him with physical assault.

86. Millea, *Ghetto Fever*, 79–81.

87. James Ralph Jr., *Northern Protest: Martin Luther King, Chicago, and the Civil Rights Movement* (Cambridge, MA: Harvard University Press, 1993), 196.

88. Knauss, *Chicago: A One-Party State*, 50–53.

89. Anderson and Pickering, *Confronting the Color Line*, 200.

90. August Meier and Elliott Rudwick, *CORE: A Study in the Civil Rights Movement, 1942–1968* (New York: Oxford University Press, 1973).

91. George Breitman, ed., *Malcolm X Speaks: Selected Speeches and Statements* (New York: Grove Press, 1965), 141.

92. Frantz Fanon, *The Wretched of the Earth*, trans. Constance Farrington (New York: Grove Press, 1963), introduction by Jean-Paul Sartre, 12–19.

Chapter 3

The Formation of the Illinois Black Panther Party

Placing the situation in its historical context is important. Chicago, black Chicago in particular, was influenced by a national mood of political activism and by the resistance to those activists. For the youthful, black radicals who became the Illinois Black Panther Party, the national experiences of the Student Nonviolent Coordinating Committee (SNCC) were probably the most significant experiences. Several founders of the Illinois Black Panther Party were from SNCC.

SNCC, EARLY 1960S

SNCC began in 1960 as a moderate, idealistic organization. Black Americans in 1960 were segregated out of the social and political life, which the majority of Americans took for granted. SNCC began wanting in, and their means of getting in was nonviolent civil disobedience, with a moral appeal to America to make it possible for black Americans to be served at ''whites-only'' restaurants, and other public facilities, and to be treated as equals on busses, trains, in schools and other segregated facilities either not available to blacks or available in circumscribed ways. SNCC wanted to dismantle racial segregation—and they wanted to see black Southerners get the right to vote. So the SNCC students originally asserted what they felt were rights denied black Americans, the right to be assimilated into the American ideals of personal, autonomous freedom— freedom to choose where to sit, where to eat, where to go to school, where to work, and how to vote.

They planned patient, nonviolent disobedience to racially discriminatory laws and customs. It was courageous in the violence-dominated Klu Klux Klan country of the 1960s South. The SNCC students were less respectful of the political order than the Southern Christian Leadership Conference (SCLC), led by Dr. Martin Luther King Jr. They were more willing to promote local leadership in their struggle. In fact, more than simply wanting those isolated choices, they also wanted democracy for poor, black Americans.[1]

From the beginning, there were seeds of radicalism in desiring democracy, in listening to the local people, and in acting courageously on their behalf. In short, SNCC showed respect for the black poor, a respect the political system of this country has not historically shown. Majority rule in the United States has usually ruled out political considerations concerning American Indians, blacks, Latinos, Asian Americans, and poor whites. Showing that respect put SNCC at odds with the political system in a way that SCLC was not. "Let our most talented in" is different from let our masses organize and, if they choose, rule themselves.

SNCC's commitment to democracy for poor blacks gave them an education. Poor people, they learned, were kept docile by force and the threat of force, in the South–and in Chicago. As SNCC activist John Perdew said in 1963, "I grew up with only an abstract, intellectual concept of race relations. I had no idea at all of any kind of violence and daily oppression that millions of people went through. That's the way I went into SNCC thinking. But then I got my ass kicked."[2] Perdew spent three months in jail for violating a law that had its origins in white Redemption Era politics, a law that was declared unconstitutional. His experience was not unusual.

What SNCC workers witnessed happening to the local leaders, whom they promoted, radicalized them also. Fannie Lou Hamer was severely beaten, D.U. Pullum was beaten, Herbert Lee was killed, Louis Allen was beaten, with the connivance of FBI officials, and later shot and killed. Their crime was the same: attempting to register to vote. Evidently, the FBI worked closely with local Southern police officers who were often violently hostile to SNCC.[3] These experiences with violence and with government connivance in that violence tended to radicalize more people than those who experienced those acts firsthand. They also tended to heighten distrust of the local as well as the federal government.[4]

SNCC students were living an experiment in trying to provide democracy for poor blacks. What they found in the process was that personal, autonomous freedom (which they had originally desired) and democracy were an unworkable combination for poor black people. Freedom required sacrifice and cooperation—and the commitment to use any means necessary to achieve it.[5] For them, as their movement continued, nonviolence became a tool, a means to an end, and it was often an ineffective tool. Once nonviolence was regarded as a tool (and not a moral principle), violence could also be seen as a tool. For example, when violence used against poor blacks intimidated them and destroyed their movement in Albany, Georgia and McComb County, Mississippi, SNCC learned from it, armed themselves for self-defense in Lowndes County, Alabama, in 1966 and formed a political organization whose voting symbol (for illiterate voters) was a black panther.[6] The local people, therefore, referred to them as the "Black Panther Party." Stokely Carmichael, a young, articulate SNCC activist, was the founder of this party, formally named the Lowndes County Freedom Organization.

Criticized by SNCC leaders in the east for not being nonviolent, Carmichael responded, "They don't do the kind of work we do, nor do they live in the areas we live in. They don't ride the highways at night."[7] Carmichael further stated that the local people were actually more ready to use guns than SNCC and that SNCC had been a restraining influence on them.[8]

By 1966, these practical considerations put SNCC to the left of Dr. King, politically. SNCC was critical of his allegiance to the Democratic Party, which, in Alabama, fought their efforts to empower poor blacks. The push for indigenous black power had awakened a latent radicalism in the poor, politically oppressed, black farmers. SNCC wanted social changes for the poor, and so did many poor people. The year was 1966, SNCC was no longer adhering to nonviolence as moral principle, and the Black Panther Party had made its first appearance—although ignored by the nation's news media.

SNCC's Carmichael coined the phrase "black power," implicitly renouncing integration as its goal and calling for a power base for black Americans. It was a shocking turn of events for liberal Americans who had envisioned a color-blind society. It was realistic, however, given the staying power of white racism. Carmichael shocked white America further, saying, "We will get this power the same way Americans got it in 1775!" *Time Magazine*, *Newsweek* and the *Saturday Evening Post* condemned him. *The Saturday Evening Post* warned SNCC to be careful. "We are all, let us face it, [white] Mississippians…"[9] And perhaps that was the trouble.

Certainly, within SNCC, white members presented a set of problems. Being inexperienced in the racial etiquette of black Southerners, they often held more automatic power than black members of SNCC–which the black members resented. The white members were often a disruptive force, whether they intended to be or not. Sometimes they tended to be arrogant and dictatorial rather than merely insensitive. SNCC, in the mid-sixties, moved toward a black nationalist perspective, not, they said, to be racist, but to avoid seeing a white agenda take over their efforts. Whites who were sincere, they said, could work on the white community's racism.[10]

On the surface, this development might appear to be a reverse racism in action. Consider, however, that black segregation was imposed and that blacks were excluded from mainstream America. Then, is it racist for blacks to unify around that label, which excludes them? Or might it not make sense to first control one's own community, then reach out for allies from a position of internal power? That was the concept that Malcolm X and Stokely Carmichael of SNCC originally preached. That Carmichael took the vision in a more racist direction is another issue. Historically, racism has been tolerated in American society far more than multi-racial unity, and Carmichael's racism would prove to be more tolerable than Huey Newton's multi-racial unity.

Urban SNCC

It was at the time, 1967, when Newark, New Jersey and the Watts community in Los Angeles broke out in ghetto riots. The spirit of the civil rights movement had touched young black people and brought the youth out of the political apathy their communities had known. Not knowing what to do to effect change, yet having expectations of a better life, young black men and women seemed determined to effect a change from years of overcrowded conditions, bad housing, underemployment and police abuse which their communities had suffered. Cases of believed police abuse were the ostensible cause of both these major riots.

The success of Southern blacks in dismantling legal segregation affected Northern urban blacks, many of them Southern "immigrants" who were angry to find that Northern cities were, in fact, if not by law, as hostile to them as the South. In fact, the destruction of the formal symbols of oppression had not changed the substance of much racial oppression–lack of political and economic power. Economic and political power had already been divided, and no one was giving up their "piece." It was apparent that black people would have to fight to get a reallocation of that power. The question to politically active black youth was how to fight.

A young man named Huey P. Newton conceived of the idea of a self-defense-oriented, political party for black people in Oakland, California. Newton was not an unusual phenomenon in the black community in regard to his intelligence, his sharp wit and his love of action. There was, however, something so brilliant and so daredevil in this young man that shocked even the most daring gangbanger.[11] The historical question naturally arises: why was this so? Perhaps his daring and his willingness to physically challenge people came from his "pretty boy" appearance, an image that consistently draws challenges to one's manhood in poor communities. Perhaps his bold daring was an intelligent adjustment to those constant challenges to his manhood. He was, nevertheless, wedded to action and yet intensely intellectual. Maybe the roots of his creative politics lay in his love of books. Clearly, Newton loved to read political treatises. That he digested Franz Fanon's books speaks pages for his intellectual abilities.[12] That he based his *actions* on Fanon indicates that his understanding of Fanon was more than superficial. Obviously challenged by some inner drive to understand these difficult political treatises, Huey Newton made them the springboard to his bold action—and that wedding of the intellectual with daring actions had startling consequences.

Newton, a college student at Merritt College, and another student there, Bobby Seale, began their political careers by arming themselves and patrolling the Oakland police, who patrolled the streets of Oakland. Newton's idea, on the surface, was to prevent police abuses of citizens.[13] Clearly, Newton was on to something a little deeper than that.

Newton thought most activists talked and did little else. He felt the movement would have to take a more active and more radical approach toward changing the conditions of the black ghetto. Newton studied Malcolm X.[14] Malcolm advised studying the historical revolutions all over the world, which sent Newton to Fanon, Mao and Lenin. Newton came with a new message in the traditional brashness of black urban youth. He walked the walk of the urban ghetto, and yet he added a political bent. Newton spearheaded a new phenomenon, politicized poor, black youth.

King's movement had begun a drift toward radicalism in the 1950s. Prior to King, college-educated young people had feared jail. Keeping away from a prison record (and from those "bad" boys who went to prison) had been a key to success. Getting black youth arrested had been a white racist tactic to defeat black men. Dr. King and student activists had turned that value around. They had gone to jail for what they believed in. They had met their "bad" brothers and found them to be people. Now they could discourse. Those acts had soldered together something of the class split in the black community. The middle-class movement began to move the urban poor. SNCC had moved that process along, working side-by-side with poor, oppressed black people. The Panther Party continued that process, promoting a political leadership of poor, urban youth.

In the spring of 1967, when the Black Panther Party for Self-Defense entered the California State Legislature, armed, supposedly, to protest a gun bill that would prohibit citizens from carrying guns openly (not simply concealed weapons), they made national headlines. Their actions consequently got national exposure. Their irreverent attitude hit the nation like a bomb. To young activists, wondering which direction would reactivate a waning movement, the Panthers provided an attention-grabbing and creative response.

To challenge the authority with a gun in one hand and a law book in the other was quite revolutionary in the history of the black community in America. As bold and aggressive as black people were with each other, they virtually never challenged the police. The leaders of SNCC initially took to it, aligning themselves with this new Black Panther Party.

This movement was almost necessarily a youth movement. Politically independent movements of the poor have never been long-lived in the United States, much less aggressive and radical movements. In Chicago, the business-political-crime triumvirate had handled that phenomenon brutally and efficiently. Who else would be so bold as to try to confront the powerful so audaciously? Black communists in Chicago in the 1940s had, for example, been virtually wiped out. Prior to them, the Garvey movement had been destroyed—as had much more moderate forms of political independence like the movement Octavious Granady represented.[15] As far as politicized, young black people were concerned, they were the only people with the backbone to accomplish the necessary task at hand. Everyone else was too intimidated to challenge the system, a system that did not respect poor people.

On April 4, 1968, Dr. Martin Luther King was killed, and Chicago's West Side went up in flames. Mayor Richard Daley issued his famous "shoot to kill" order, and some nine black people were killed in that riot.[16]

Significantly, the South Side had had no riot–although National Guard Units did not appreciate the difference between the two ghettoes and sent truckloads of troops riding through them both.

Two months later, Bobby Rush, Bob Brown and a few other SNCC activists began touring local city college campuses, recruiting for a branch of the Black Panther Party in Chicago.[17]

Chicago was just two months away from having its own branch of the Black Panther Party.

THE INTELLECTUAL BASE

First, young people read Malcolm X:

> The Chinese Revolution--they wanted land. They threw the British out, along with the Uncle Tom Chinese. Yes, they did. They set a good example. When I was in prison, I read an article–don't be shocked when I say that I was in prison. You're still in prison. That's what America means. Prison! When I was in prison, I read an article in Life Magazine showing a little Chinese girl, nine years old; her father was on his hands and knees, and she was pulling the trigger because he was an Uncle Torn Chinaman. When they had their revolution over there, they wiped out a whole generation of Uncle Toms…No more Uncle Toms in China. And now it is one of the roughest, most feared countries on this earth–by the white man.

> Of all our studies, history is best qualified to reward our research. And when you see you have problems, all you have to do is examine the historic method used all over the world by others who have problems similar to yours. Once you see how they got theirs straight, you know how you can get yours straight…In Algeria, a revolution took place. The Algerians were revolutionists…[18]

Young black activists followed Malcolm X's suggestion and looked at recent successful opposition to European dominance, found their examples in the writings of Mao Tse-tung of China, Franz Fanon of Algeria and Ché Guevara of Cuba. Fanon, in particular, as a black, but European-educated Algerian who had renounced his Europeanized persona and returned to his native Algeria to side with the "natives," held a position they regarded as similar to their own. Black youth admired Mao and Fanon because they were successful, and these activists had not seen what was regarded as success domestically. So, following the lead of Newton in Oakland, Bobby Rush, Bob Brown, Henry English, and other Chicago Panthers read Mao and Fanon and moved with that revolutionary spirit in Chicago, as Chicago SNCC became the Illinois Black Panther Party.

Fred Hampton

Bobby Rush was the originator of the move to form an Illinois Black Panther Party. However, Rush, a dogged, unexpressive, almost inarticulate person, might have had a very different, perhaps obscure life if he had not introduced the Party to a spirited, personable, articulate 20-year-old named Fred Hampton. Hampton was a thoughtful, ambitious young man who knew what he wanted to do early in life. He wanted to be a lawyer and a fighter for his people.[19] Like Huey Newton, he was an avid reader. Unlike Newton, Hampton consciously worked at making himself into a persuasive and articulate speaker. He studied the speeches of Malcolm X and Dr. King.[20] Like Newton, Fred Hampton had little or no fear of physical confrontations; he was more inclined to persuasion, but a warrior nonetheless. He would have to be as a leader in this Illinois Black Panther Party, for there were some tough warriors of the streets in the Party, who were not easily led, but were in need of leadership.

Hampton hoped to get a law degree one day, but activism held a fascination for him. He had joined the NAACP in 1966, in Maywood, and was made president of its West Suburban Youth Council.[21]

Residents of Maywood who knew Hampton in his pre-Panther days describe him as a remarkable young man. He had been known to defuse a potential riot in Maywood, capture the spirit of angry black youth, and lead them on a nonviolent march through the streets of Maywood, 500 strong, protesting their exclusion from the neighborhood swimming pool. White citizens had also enlisted him to talk with white students about their racism. Hampton had confronted them, without losing them, and instead let them see their actions through a black perspective. They ended up acknowledging they had not been without prejudice.[22]

It was not Bobby Rush who won Hampton over to the philosophy of the Black Panther Party, but a young man from the Los Angeles Panthers, one of Alprentice "Bunchy" Carter's warriors.[23] In 1968, however, Lennie Eggleston, the L.A. Panther touring Chicago on speaking engagements for the Panthers, met and talked with Hampton at great length.[24]

Before talking with Lennie Eggleston, Hampton considered himself a black nationalist and regarded racial unity as fundamental, and poor whites as natural adversaries. In the discussion, Eggleston agreed with Hampton that poor whites were racist, but asserted that black people should not let others define who was and who was not an ally. Black people, although a poor minority, still had the power to define their own reality, Eggleston argued. Black people did not have to give in to a racist reality. He said black people could use class solidarity as a tool to redefine the situation. We (Blacks) could unite the poor—if we believed we could—and revolutionize America. Eggleston's argument was low-key, patient and persistent, and it won Hampton over. The idea of redefining poor people related very strongly to his Maywood experiences. By the end of their discussions, Fred Hampton agreed that a movement that transcended race was revolutionary and original. It was a creative idea, particularly among black youth in an alienated ghetto. Imagine the possibilities of the poorest and most alienated leading a revolution of the poor, warriors from all the "tribes" uniting to fight those in charge.[25]

The lyrics of the song read, "Youth and truth are making love, dig it for a starter. Dying young is hard to take, [but] selling out is harder."[26] Sly and the Family Stone were singing the feelings of the radicals of the 1960s. The year 1968 was a year of "Stop the War!" or even, "Bring the War Home!" Radical American students questioned the necessity for foreign wars, and the validity of capitalism, even the rationale behind race prejudice. Sly and the Family Stone, a multi-ethnic, bi-gender band, singing a new sound, with an optimistic vision of what America could be. The Black Panther Party was a radical political version of that same optimism. The Panthers were not out to simply unify the black ghetto; they wanted to revolutionize the entire society. They were optimistic to the point of naivete.

The fact is a big change had occurred in American society. Several million disenfranchised Americans were coming into the political process of voting. What other power would they get? What other changes would be wrought? Change, student unrest, and questioning produced the atmosphere in which people, young people in particular, wanted to push the changes as far as they could. Why not have a foreign policy run by the people? Why not give more power to the people? This American nation is a democracy, it was said, so why not let democratic ideals rule? In this atmosphere, when Huey Newton said "seize the time!" people responded. Would the United States undergo a revolution? Young intellectuals thought it just might. If the revolution took place, would the black radicals lead it? Many young activists thought these were the correct questions to be asking at that time.[27]

The Formation of the Illinois (Chicago) Black Panther Party

Weeks after Dr. King was assassinated, black activist Phil Cohran held a black leadership conference in Chicago, and young radical thinkers responded.[28] At an enthusiastic rally of several hundred young people, held at the Afro-Arts Theater on 39th Street and Drexel Avenue—later famous as "The Fort" of the Black P. Stone Nation—Bobby Rush was there, searching for a dynamic speaker to help build the Illinois chapter of the Black Panther Party. He had met Fred Hampton one week earlier and briefly left the meeting to call him. Hampton agreed to join the organization and serve as its chairman.

At the same approximate time, on the West Side of Chicago, another Black Panther Party was forming in the East Garfield area. They were younger members of the Deacons and local young adults, some out of the Vice Lords. They were led by Drew Ferguson and Jewel Cook, young residents of the area. In August, they held a rally at the Senate Theater on Madison at Kedzie Avenue. They leafleted their neighborhood and produced a good crowd, and somehow the SNCC-formed Panthers heard about their rally and arrived, some twenty of them, led by Bobby Rush and Bob Brown, both formerly active in the Chicago Freedom Movement.[29] The two groups met that afternoon and decided to combine.[30]

The FBI described Bob Brown at this time as "extremely militant" and someone they needed to "remove from the scene through some form of legal or police action."[31] It is noteworthy that police action and legal actions are not considered equivalent in this memo. At the time, the FBI also had a file on Fred Hampton.

The neighborhood they were in heavily influenced the spirit in these formative days of the Illinois Black Panther Party, home to thousands of Southern-born and raised Chicagoans, who still had the old community ways of the South in them. The Panthers went out into the streets, into the pool halls and the taverns and nightclubs and playgrounds and talked about revolution. In addition, they talked about respecting black women, and staying in school and living a righteous life. While the Panthers preached not to accept abuse, they also preached not to give abuse. They babysat children, and helped old folks with their groceries, and they showed blatant disrespect to the police. They believed they had to set an example of fearlessness and intolerance of abusive behavior. It was something many of them had wanted to do all their young lives. Now they had an organization to do it in, express their spirit of community, and set the wayward straight.[32] There was the same motive in them that led many people into the ministry or into becoming police officers(!).

The phraseology they used, however, did not come from the Bible, but from *The Quotations from Chairman Mao Tse-tung*. Mao and the Chinese Communists had thrown off the imperialist powers, so they were considered a valid guide. Mao's advice was in easy phrases: "All power to the People," "The spirit of man is greater than Man's technology," "The masses are the real heroes," "The masses have a potentially inexhaustible enthusiasm for socialism," "The people, and the people alone, are the motive force in the making of world history." They used the phrases and translated them into the jargon of the streets. They were attempting to build the people's spirits up while setting an example of service. The words emboldened them as they patrolled the streets of a tough, poor community. The Panthers did not tolerate disrespect in their faces, and interfered with those economics of the poor that tear down self-respect. The Panthers would stop a woman from selling her body, lecture her, interfere with her trade, threaten her pimp, order drug dealers off the streets, and beat them up if they did not heed a warning.[33] They were walking the streets of Miles Square (their immediate locale), interfering with disrespect, and they were immediately popular. Every time they went out, they came back with recruits. Their actions were bold, daring and positive. They captured the imagination of those who dreamed of saving their community in dramatic ways.

While their approach may have had ideological roots in Fanon and Mao, at least from the intellectuals, the way they went about it was, as the locals described it, a "down-home" response to building people up. As local community leader Nancy Jefferson said, "The Black Panthers were like the old-time men. They were not afraid to put somebody straight."[34] Mrs. Jefferson, Director of the Mid-West Community Council, twenty-five years senior to the average Panther, admired them on an emotional level. Not only did she like their spirit and their self-respect, she saw them as having the character that was lacking in many of the young people who go around stealing from one another. The Panther appeal was largely on that emotion-spirit level. That is why Joe Shaw joined the Panthers at nineteen. He felt they were doing right, and they were his "homeboys." Fred Hampton and he were from the same small town in Louisiana.[35] Joe Shaw, like scores of local young adults, did not know a lot about socialism, nor Marxism, nor about Mao nor Fanon, but he felt that the Panthers' hearts were right.[36]

PANTHER PARTY STRUCTURE

The Black Panther Party was organized, in form, like the Chinese Communist Party, with no single leader, but a Central Committee. Branches and chapters, including the Illinois Chapter, followed that same organization, but their offices reflected the Oakland Headquarters' supremacy by labeling the local officers deputy officers. While the Oakland Panther Party had a Minister of Defense, the Illinois Chapter had a Deputy Minister of Defense, who was Bobby Rush.

The Illinois Deputy Central Committee consisted of a Deputy Chairman, Fred Hampton, who acted as the spokesperson for the Central Committee. There were also Deputy Ministers of Defense, Education, Information, Culture, Finance and Labor. These ministers made decisions for the organization jointly. They included Bobby Rush, strong-willed, but shy, almost inarticulate, while evidently motivated by a sincere belief in the Party. Billy Brooks, reputedly hard and hot-tempered, but in reality, that hardness was a bluff, hiding an analytical mind and a good sense of humor. The other members of the Central Committee were Rufus Walls, Deputy Minister of Information; Alvino Sheen, Deputy Minister of Finance; and Ann Campbell, Communications Secretary. And there were three Field Lieutenants–Jewel Cook, Bobby Lee, and Joan Gray. Tall, attractive Yvonne King, Deputy Minister of Labor, was, like many of the Panthers, both street smart and a prodigious reader. The women all tended to be personable, well-read and intellectual people, more so than the men, who appeared to be hard, analytical and adept at reading a person's face, but not so much into books.[37]

These young people were voted into office by their peers on the basis of their street smarts. They were respected, which made for good morale, but they had to create their jobs.[38]

Each Deputy Minister was responsible for a cadre of individual Party members, for seeing that they carried out their responsibilities. Each Party member was assigned to a cadre. Every Party member had a job to do, though all shared in two basic tasks: 1) Selling the Black Panther

Community News every day, and 2) helping with the Free Breakfast for Children programs organized that year. Decisions were voted on; one person, one vote. They could appeal decisions, but until the appeal was made, the decision had to be obeyed. Discipline was physical. If a Party member was late for a meeting or failed to carry out an assignment, it meant a hard slap in the face for the women and a hard kick in the butt for the men. According to Yvonne King, who took one hard slap in the face, physical punishment was effective. She said it made the Black Panther Party the most reliable organization she has ever worked in.[39] Since discipline was evenhanded and determined by popularly elected leaders, morale remained high, as long as there was that leadership.[40]

In its first three or four months, the Illinois Panther Party's growth was phenomenal. It grew from some forty original members to well over 300, not to mention a few runaway adolescents who ran away from home to be "like the Panthers," as one put it, "one hundred percent for the people!"[41] Many Party members had not expected this sudden popularity. It was, however, strictly local. The great majority of people in Chicago still did not know who they were, except for what the news media said, and it seemed they were some sort of new gang, or was that the Blackstone Rangers? People who were not of the neighborhood often mixed them up.

BLACK CHICAGO AND THE PANTHER STYLE

In 1968, black men and women wore the "natural" as a hairstyle and a political statement. In contrast to the processing oils and acids that blacks had been using to make their hair look like white people, the idea was that black people no longer had to strive to be white. One could be oneself–whoever that was. Natural was not just a style; it was a statement. It meant you be you, and that is good enough. The Black Panther Party took to the statement wholeheartedly. Just being exactly who one was should be enough for the rest of American society. That philosophy could and did extend beyond hair into language.

The most common word heard up and down the streets of the black ghetto was "mothafuckah." So as often as not, when one heard the Panthers make a statement, it was punctuated with that word. For example, "We are revolutionaries, mothafuckah!" When the Panthers were criticized about their language, they decided the rest of America could take it or leave it, but that was who they were. They often spoke in hyperbole. "Blood to the horse's brow! And woe be unto those who cannot swim!" was a common expression at Panther headquarters.[42] The phrase came from Chairman Mao and Party members, having to read Mao and Fanon, found that Mao had some catchy phrases that lent themselves to the verbal language easily. It was, however, not the exact meaning behind the phrase but the spirit it seemed to arouse, which made a Maoistic phrase popular. If the phrase was bold, audacious and exuberant, the Panthers used it. Examples include, "Political power comes from the barrel of a gun!" "The spirit of man is greater than Man's technology!" "Dare to struggle, dare to win!" Such phrase-taking bordered dangerous ground, with the white media, yet the Panthers felt to back off a phrase was deflating, the challenge was to use it. Therefore, when Mao said, "wipe out some, get some satisfaction; wipe out more, get more satisfaction; wipe out the whole lot, complete satisfaction."[43] Hampton used it. Calling the police "the pigs" was attitudinally far removed from calling them "the man," which was a common term prior to the Panthers. Pig was a term originated by the Panthers. Calling for their death, as in "Off the Pigs!" was the joy of hyperbole.

Black Chicago youth had dressed in two styles in the 1950s and 60s, reflecting the class division in the black community. These two styles were known as "gouster" and "Ivy Leaguer." The Ivy League style consisted of dress shirts, usually "Brooks Brothers," skinny ties, creased and rather tight pants and oxfords. The gouster style was baggy trousers, baggy "Van-Ion" shirts, wide-brimmed hats and suspenders, sometimes with a long chain hanging from the pocket. They called themselves "gousters," and they aspired to gaining riches on the street, while "Ivy leaguers" were college-bound. The styles were fading as of 1968, and the Panthers pushed them on their way out. An entire new world was opening up to black youth, and the working-class youth were leading the way into it. Whichever way it went, there was a pride that transcended class, and a soldering of the class rift, which was pushing it out. There was an appreciation of the strength of poor black culture that did not imitate white America. History had moved the need for Ivy League and gouster out.

All over black Chicago, people stopped "slapping five" (hitting each other's open hand) and began "giving the fist." That fist meant "Black Power!" That fist in the air gave people a rush, a kind of high.

The Panthers felt they were on a high. "We high off [of] the people!" Fred Hampton used to say.[44] The spirit was infectious around the Panther Party in its first year. If one stayed around them, one would eventually want to serve the people, too. Pimps stopped pimping to serve the people, gang-bangers quit the gangs and joined the Panthers. There was a hope in the air, and an idea that the people could do anything.[45]

The Panthers had a set of rules on how to deal with the people, and they were essentially the same rules the Chinese Communist Party professed to use. No Party member was to steal anything, no matter how small, from the people. (Stealing from downtown department stores was another matter entirely.) They were not to be intoxicated or smoke "weed" while on duty. They were to be polite at all times. When they were arrested, they were to give no information except their name and address. They were not to accept any money from the government, and they were each to submit in writing what they had done at the end of each day.[46]

The Panther's spirit was tinged with anger. Dr. King had been killed, and the ghetto smoldered from that, and the living conditions, which had not changed in the years of the Civil Rights Movement. These young black people believed that those in charge had laid down the gauntlet and said, there are some things poor black people will not get–basically, political power and the respect that comes with it. In Chicago, one could add an exclamation point to that challenge, for the Democratic Machine was undemocratic when it came to poor and black people and strangled independent political and economic activities not under its control. The enemy for West Siders was clearly defined: the politician-mob-police triumvirate. The Panther Party was a direct challenge to that powerful trio and showed sufficient courage to take on that enemy. They did not have the political knowledge yet, but they had the spirit.

> You can see that spirit and that exuberant high of the Panthers, in Hampton's description of his citizens' arrest of a Chicago police officer:
>
> We just got back from the South Side. We went out there–we went out there, and we got to arguing with a pig and the pig got to arguing–he said, 'Well, Chairman Fred, you supposed to be so bad, why don't you go and shoot some of those policemen? You always talking about you got your guns and got this, why don't you go shoot some of them?'
>
> And I said, 'You've just broken a rule. As a matter of fact, even though you have on a uniform, it doesn't make me any difference. Because I don't care if you got on nine uniforms

and 100 badges. When you step outside the realm of legality and into the realm of illegality, then I feel that you should be arrested.'

And I told him, 'You being what they call the law of entrapment, you tried to incite me to commit a crime, you tried to make me do something that was wrong. You encouraged me, you tried to incite me to shoot a pig. And that ain't cool, brother. You know the law, don't you?

I told him, 'You gotta get your hands up against the wall. We're gonna do what they call a citizen's arrest.' This fool didn't know what this is. I said, 'Now you be just as calm as you can and don't make too many quick moves, 'cause we don't want to have to hit you.'

And I told him, *like they always tell us*, [emphasis added] I told him, 'Well, I'm here to protect you. Don't worry about a thing. I'm here for your benefit.' So then I sent another brother to call the pigs—you gotta do that in a citizen's arrest...and what happened? All those people were out there on 63rd Street... They were around there laughing and talking with me while I was making the arrest...So the next time the pig comes on 73rd Street (and breaks the law) because of the thing our Minister of Defense calls observation and participation, that pig might be arrested by anybody.[47]

This activity was typical of the Black Panther Party's attitude and spirit, provoking the police to act their worst (or their best, if they chose to ignore the provocation) while making some fundamental points about law officers: 1) that police should be subject to the law. (From the experience of the average West Sider, police acted as if they were above the law and were ignorant of citizens' rights). And 2) when the police were in violation of the law, they should suffer the same consequences everyone else does.

SUMMATION

The Illinois Black Panther Party was initially the expression of an attitude of determination to achieve political power in the hands of local young adults. It was an expression of anger directed at the political forces that kept poor and black people relatively powerless in this Chicago. It had very little knowledge about how the various economic and political institutions of the city worked to achieve that emasculation of the poor. It had, however, struck a nerve simply by boldly stating its disrespect for a system disrespectful of poor people.

The Illinois Panthers planned to educate the people, simply by boldly behaving as if Chicago were a democracy and they had the rights of middle-class suburbanites planning an independent revolutionary movement, challenging the authority so that the political authority would reveal its contempt for the people.

Their potential was in their sincerity, their uncompromising stance and their accurate focus on the enemy. The Panthers, still wanting the changes denied by peaceful, nonviolent protest, were about to try to take that power, using any means necessary.

This radical movement was a youthful, grassroots phenomenon in Chicago, born with simple faith in the people of the community. Without using any sophisticated analysis but with the gut feeling of youth, they called for revolution. With little knowledge of the institutions of control, and no inside connections to them, but with plenty of street knowledge, the next move was obvious–politicize and organize the everyday people.

Notes

1. Clayborne Carson, *In Struggle: SNCC and the Black Awakening of the 1960s* (Cambridge, MA: Harvard University Press, 1981), 35–55.
2. Carson, *In Struggle*, 73.
3. Carson, *In Struggle*, 48–49, 85.
4. Carson, *In Struggle*, 121–122.
5. Carson, *In Struggle*, 126–129.
6. Robert Conot, *Rivers of Blood, Years of Darkness* (New York: William Morrow, 1968), 217.
7. Carson, *In Struggle*, 164.
8. Carson, *In Struggle*, 165.
9. Carson, *In Struggle*, 221.
10. Carson, *In Struggle*, 215–218.
11. David Hilliard, *This Side of Glory: The Autobiography of David Hilliard and the Story of the Black Panther Party* (Boston: Little, Brown, 1993), 118–119.
12. Hilliard, *This Side of Glory*, 6.
13. Bobby Seale, *Seize the Time: The Story of the Black Panther Party and Huey P. Newton* (New York: Random House, 1970), 23.
14. George Breitman, ed., *Malcolm X Speaks: Selected Speeches and Statements* (New York: Grove Press, 1965), 8–9.
15. The Granady assassination had been discussed earlier.
16. Len O'Connor, *Clout: Mayor Daley and His City* (New York: Avon Books, 1975), 203. O'Connor quotes Daley as stating: "I told [Police Superintendent] Conlisk to issue an order to police to shoot to maim or cripple any looters… to shoot arsonists on sight."
17. Interview with Bobby Rush, former deputy minister of defense, Illinois Black Panther Party, April 12, 1982.
18. Breitman, ed., *Malcolm X Speaks*, 8.
19. Interview with Akua Njeri (formerly Deborah Johnson), July 12, 1988.
20. Njeri interview.
21. Interview with Joan Elbert, president of the Lutheran Human Relations Association of Maywood, Illinois, February 1981. Elbert was a neighbor of the Hampton family and had known them for several years.
22. Elbert interview.
23. Alprentice "Bunchy" Carter was a street activist who later became a leader in the Black Panther Party. He was killed by members of Ron Karenga's US Organization.
24. Elbert interview.
25. Elbert interview.
26. "Thank You (Falettinme Be Mice Elf Agin)," Sly and the Family Stone,

Flower Productions, 1968.
27. Michael Gray, *American Revolution II* (film). For a view of radical youth in Chicago during 1968, this film contains significant footage of young activists discussing revolutionary politics. Harold Washington Library Center (Chicago), Media Collection.
28. Interview with Phil Cohran, political activist, July 1, 1981.
29. Interview with Jewel Cook, Billy Brooks, and Cleveland Cook, August 11, 1982.
30. Interviews with founding members of the Illinois Black Panther Party, including Henry English, Jewel Cook, Billy Brooks, Bobby Rush, and Cleveland Cook, July–August 1982.
31. Federal Bureau of Investigation, SAC Chicago (157-2209), Counterintelligence Program, Black Nationalist Hate Groups, memorandum dated November 7, 1968. The memo notes: "Chicago SNCC is virtually defunct. Chicago division informant who was key SNCC informant is now key Black Panther informant."
32. Interviews with Henry English, Yvonne King, Jewel Cook, Billy Brooks, and Bobby Rush.
33. Same as above. When interviewees described these outings, their expressions suggested pride and sincerity.
34. Interview with Nancy Jefferson, director of the Midwest Community Council, June 3, 1981.
35. Interview with Joseph Shaw, May 14, 1995.
36. Jefferson interview.
37. Author's assessment based on several interviews with the individuals mentioned above.
38. Interviews with Illinois Black Panther Party members Willie Calvin, Joan McCarty, and Gregory Garrett.
39. Interview with Yvonne King, April 6, 1982.
40. Summary opinion drawn from interviews with Illinois Black Panther Party members.
41. Brooks interview.
42. Interview with Joan McCarty, former Illinois Black Panther Party member, July 17, 1985.
43. Mao Tse-tung, *Quotations from Chairman Mao Tse-tung* (Peking: Foreign Languages Press, 1967), 84.
44. Michael Gray and Howard Alk, producers, *The Murder of Fred Hampton* (film), 1969.
45. Interviews with Patricia Berg of the National Black Draft Counselors, July 1972, and Deidre Prince, former volunteer with the Illinois Black Panther Party, August 1969.

46. G. Louis Heath, *Off the Pigs! The History and Literature of the Black Panther Party* (Metuchen, NJ: Scarecrow Press, 1976), 85–86.
47. Fred Hampton, speech published in *Vita Wa Watu: A New Afrikan Theoretical Journal*, 3.

Chapter 4

Characterizing the Illinois Black Panthers

"The rage of the oppressed is never the same as the rage of the
privileged. One group can change their lot only by changing
the system; the other hopes to be rewarded within the
system."[1] Bell Hooks, *Killing Rage/Ending Racism*

Who were the Panthers? What did the members of the Illinois Black
Panther Party attempt to do? What was their ultimate purpose? What
were their immediate goals? How did they go about attempting to achieve
these goals? This chapter will focus on these questions, and in so doing,
reveal the character of the Illinois (Chicago) Black Panther Party of the
years from 1968 to 1970.

The Black Panther Party's ultimate goal, as its Chicago spokesperson
Fred Hampton saw it, was the same as Dr. King's: to end racial and class
oppression. Why did this send the Party in a revolutionary direction?
Hampton explains the Panther political thought on this issue when he
spoke:

> ...we never negated the fact that there was racism in America,
> but we said that the by-product, what comes off of capitalism,
> that happens to be racism. That capitalism comes first, and
> next is racism. That when they brought slaves over here, it was
> to make money. So, first, the idea came that we want to make
> money, then slaves came in order to make that money. That
> means that capitalism had to, through historical fact, racism

had to come from capitalism. It had to be capitalism first, and racism was a by-product of that…

And, we understand. You know, a lot of people have hang-ups with the Party because the Party talks about a class struggle. And, the people that have those hang-ups are opportunists… and they use these things as an excuse…so they say…Well, I can't deal with the Panther Party because the Panthers are engrossed with dealing with oppressor country radicals, or white people, or hunkies. We say primarily that the priority of this struggle is class. That Marx, and Lenin, and Ché Guevara and Mao Tse-tung and anybody else that has ever said or known or practiced anything about revolution, always said that a revolution is a class struggle…[2]

Out of this theory, taken from Mao, Fanon, Marx and Lenin came the unique coalition politics of the Illinois Panthers. In the early months of 1969, the Illinois Black Panther Party met and attempted alliances with five youth groups from different racial, ethnic and class backgrounds in a city where segregation and social mores had precluded that type of alliance building. These groups were: the Black P. Stone Nation, a South Side gang/club; the Students for a Democratic Society, a revolutionary political club of largely white college students; a Puerto Rican gang/club, which, like the P. Stone Nation, was developing a social conscience, known as the Young Lords,[3] and a club of young Appalachian migrants called the Young Patriots. The Panthers also aligned with a club of the young "greaser" crowd from the Logan Square area, who called themselves Rising Up Angry.

At the same time, these young black men and women, the members of the Illinois Black Panther Party, were risking their personal safety, going into "foreign" segregated neighborhoods to create alliances, they also began two social service programs in their own neighborhood. These programs were the "Free Breakfast for Children Program" and the "People's Free Medical Clinic."

The Black Panther Party and Black Gangs in Chicago

The black gangs of Chicago, the Blackstone Rangers (later known as the Black P. Stone Nation, then the El Rukns) in particular, had already entered the world of politics when they began to receive federal money after the black riots of 1967. The federal government looked for a means to control black gangs in order to prevent riots.[4] Evidence suggests, however, that the Chicago city government was looking for ways to destroy black gangs. In the fall of 1967, for example, there had been more than fifty young people known to have been shot in gang incidents in Chicago. It was not until the Spring of 1968, however, when the largest gang in the city, the Blackstone Rangers, with at least three thousand members, began to get money from the federal government–money not controlled by City Hall–that they ran into serious trouble.[5] Historically, who had controlled where federal money is spent in Chicago has been a sensitive issue with the Cook County Democratic Party. There was knowledgeable speculation that because funds to the Rangers, through the U.S. Office of Economic Opportunity, were not under the control of the Daley-led Democratic Party, and because the Rangers were beginning to offer services to their community, like the Democratic Party did, that Mayor Daley saw them as potential competition.[6] Mayor Daley's own background in the Irish gang/club, known as the Hamburg Club, may have led his thoughts in that direction.

The Blackstone Rangers, which changed its name to the Black P. Stone Nation in 1968, was becoming involved in city politics. With urging from the Rev. Jesse Jackson, the gang took up the fight to get black men into the all-white trade unions, and helped him block construction sites on the black South Side. Burly, white workers had run Rev. Jackson and his protesters off a site, and so they had come back with the P. Stone members, who ran the unionized construction workers from that site, and others, with bats, pipes and bricks.[7]

Scores of P. Stones then went with Rev. Jackson to the construction site of the University of Illinois and, when Rev. Jackson decided to back off from a confrontation, the Stones blocked his way out, and would not let him get back in his car, forcing him to go through with the action he had proposed.[8] This was a strong indication that, although he had invited them into the movement, they were not under Rev Jackson's control. Three thousand black kids moving into politics were a threat to the status quo. On the other hand, to the Illinois Black Panther Party, this political activity meant they were potential allies.

In January of 1969, the P. Stone Nation, located on the South Side, and the largely West Side Black Panther Party held a meeting. The meeting was impromptu, precipitated by the shooting of a member of the Panther Party selling *The Black Panther Community News* in the Woodlawn neighborhood, P. Stone Nation "Territory."[9] The Panther Party used the incident to take thirty armed Panthers over to P. Stone Nation headquarters. Six cars loaded with armed Panthers drove down the Eisenhower expressway and arrived at the Stones' headquarters to make an impression on the Stones. Jeff Fort, an unusually charismatic personality among gangbangers, brought his armament out on walkie-talkie command, new carbines, pistols and shotguns, in the hands of about one hundred teens. Jeff Fort was known for his amazing ability to get his young followers to commit brazen acts of lethal violence, even over the phone, from jail. These recorded "hits" would be his undoing in later years, but as of 1969, he may have been the most independent of the black poor in Chicago.[10] Fort did not impress the Panthers, however, because they were determined not to be impressed, armed with a cause they believed in, and probably convinced they were as tough or tougher than any South Siders. (The warriors in the Panther Party were largely West Siders. As has been shown, the West Siders came with a different history.) The Panther leaders called for an end to gang violence, the right to sell their newspaper anywhere and that the P. Stone Nation enlist into the Black Panther Party and take up socialism and revolution.[11]

The Stones agreed to the Panthers' right to sell their newspapers, but nothing else. The Stones were out to make money, not to share it, and socialism sounded like a sharing process to them.[12] They were impressed, however, that someone from the legitimate world had reached out to them. They recognized that the Illinois Panther Party was run by some sincere people and that the Panthers had acknowledged them.[13] The Illinois Panthers attempted to redeem the Stones without attacking their right to be organized. By contrast, the Chicago social and law enforcement systems regarded them as unredeemable and were determined to destroy them as an organization.

While the Illinois Black Panther Party attempted to get a cease-fire between the P. Stone Nation and their South Side rivals, the Black Gangster Disciple Nation, the political system's harassment of the Stones intensified. Stones from the east end of the South Side were picked up by police and dropped off in the Black Disciple neighborhood west of Cottage Grove Avenue. The YMCA protested that the Stones were running social service programs and that activity should be denied them.[14] The newly formed Gang Intelligence Unit of the Chicago Police Department began arresting any black males found on the streets of Woodlawn. At the same time, the local Woodlawn Organization (TWO) and the Stones began a serious dialogue about improving the community.[15] The following interview of the Gang Intelligence Unit's head, Edward Buckney, is a good sample of the establishment's thinking on the subject of this gang:

> QUESTION: How can other social agencies work with gangs?
>
> BUCKNEY: They can't.
>
> QUESTION: Then who can work with the gangs?
>
> BUCKNEY: The police.
>
> QUESTION: How can churches and other groups help the police work with gangs?
>
> BUCKNEY: They can't.
>
> QUESTION: Of the many different efforts now being made in Chicago to deal with gangs, which has been the most helpful to the police?
>
> BUCKNEY: The formation of the Gang Intelligence Unit.
> QUESTION: What can be done about the gangs?
>
> BUCKNEY: They must be broken up.[16]

The *Chicago Tribune* ran a series on their front pages of supposed sex orgies and other illegal activities at the job sites where the members of the P. Stone Nation were employed. The *Tribune* claimed to be outraged that known gang members ran these job programs.[17] The fact that the police never arrested anyone for these acts, each supposedly committed by a named person, with a supposed eyewitness, seems to invalidate the newspaper's accuracy. The attitude of the police, the YMCA and the *Chicago Tribune* centered exclusively on breaking up this particular gang (the one developing a social program)–so that organized crime in Woodlawn gave way to less organized crime.

Clearly, crime itself, drug trafficking principally, continued to flourish in the aftermath of the P. Stone Nation's destruction. This destruction occurred over the next decade as the police and the federal government kept a steady pressure on P. Stones' breakup. The "Stones" were violent, even murderously so, dealing almost exclusively in illegal activities, yet they had something of a social conscience. The P. Stone Nation (or El

Rukns, as they later called themselves) had evidently not allowed crack-cocaine to come into their neighborhood. Once they were destroyed, the drug known as "crack" soon flooded the Southeast Side of Chicago.[18]

The question has to be asked: had the Panther Party redeemed the gang and brought them into a revolutionary youth movement, what would the eventual outcome have been, particularly in terms of crime in that neighborhood? A second, but as significant question is, was the purpose of the busting up of this gang a political one? That is to say, were they made a target because they dared to demonstrate a social conscience? After all, the Black Disciples (later known as the Black Gangster Disciple Nation), virtually next door, were allowed to flourish—until they too involved themselves in city politics through the organization of the 1990s, 21st Century Vote. Once they made that political move, they too came under attack, though they had flourished virtually untouched from the 1960s through the 1980s.

In 1969, the Illinois Black Panther Party negotiated with the three largest gangs in Chicago: the Black P. Stone Nation, the Black Gangster Disciple Nation, and the Conservative Vice Lords, but achieved no alliances. However, they did have some success in their attempts. They exposed these wayward youths to a group of sincere, pro-community young adults, with a new way of looking at the current situation they were in, and gave them a look at a revolutionary perspective. Hampton warned them that they would not be allowed to exist as a legitimate organization outside the control of the establishment.[19] These gang members were also treated with respect by Panthers and, consequently, became keen observers of the Panther Party's experiences. When, later that year, the police intensified their harassment of the Illinois Black Panther Party, and the Party responded with armed self-defense, a message was sent across youthful, black Chicago. For while the gangbangers fought and killed each other without much thought, they stayed clear of the police. The Black Panther Party felt no regrets about fighting anyone who disrespected them, most pointedly the police. The message they sent was one of *self-respect*, the strong point of Panther politics.

Black Panthers as Warriors

The Panthers who went south with Hampton to talk with the Stones were the warriors, young men like Jewel Cook, formerly of the Deacons for Defense and Justice, Drew Ferguson, a redeemed gangbanger from the

Conservative Vice Lords, and Vietnam War veterans Willie Calvin and Henry English. They had their principles of what was right and wrong, and they had an ethical code: Serve the People, straight from the South, by way of the West Side of Chicago, paying respects to Mao Tse-tung, in the Black Panther Party. When they looked the Stones in the eye and said, "Stop killing other black folks," their sincerity and their toughness were obvious.[20]

There was more to the Illinois Panthers than the warriors. There were some very well-read intellectuals like Fred Hampton, Bob Brown, Bobby Lee, Joan and Michael McCarty, Joan Gray, Yvonne King, Kassandra Watson, Gregory Garrett and Lynn French. In 1969, you seldom saw these young 19 to 22-year-olds without a book in their pocket. They had a popular book at the time on how to win people over, and other books on liberation struggles around the globe.[21]

Yvonne King later became a lawyer and helped create a law school.[22] Joan Gray was to create a dance theater.[23] Kassandra Watson became an official with City Hall, then a judge. Lynn French became an official in the D.C. Housing Department.[24] In 1969, all of them were in the Illinois Black Panther Party and gave it a dimension beyond its warrior image.

The Illinois Black Panther Party not only was able to deal with the toughest black youth in the city but also began a coalition among white, black and Latino youth, intellectuals and working class. This Rainbow Coalition, as the Deputy Chairman of the Illinois Panthers, Fred Hampton, called it, was a good ten years ahead of Rev. Jesse Jackson's coalition of the same name.

Here was a unique event in the history of black Chicago, a political coalition that not only respected the black community but was led by a black leadership. In the same month that Fred Hampton and company went to pay a visit to the Black P. Stone Nation, Panther Field Lieutenant Bobby Lee went to Uptown, a poor white neighborhood, to discuss a coalition between the Illinois Black Panther Party and a neighborhood youth group known as the Young Patriots.[25]

The Young Patriots were immigrants from the coal mines of West Virginia and Tennessee who were struggling to better their community. They were proud of their Southern heritage. One could hardly expect these two historic antagonists, poor Southern whites and poor Southern blacks, to get along. However, with Panther Bobby Lee at the helm of this coalition, and Panther/Marxist politics as their guide, they achieved just that. By that spring, 1969, the Young Patriots ran a Free Breakfast for

Children program, modeled after the Panther Party programs.[26]

About that same time, early 1969, a carload of white boys from the Logan Square area drove over to the heart of the black West Side to meet the Panthers. These young men (and women) were forming their own organization, based on the Panther politics of revolution and class solidarity, and called themselves Rising Up Angry. They preached revolution and the need for socialism, and began their own newspaper, *Rising Up Angry*, imitating the Panther paper but using the street vernacular of the white North Side. The paper poked fun at "da Mayor" and "da cops." This was Rising Up Angry's first trip to Panther headquarters, and the local police did not know what to make of them.

Who had ever heard of a gang of white boys coming en masse to the black ghetto? That kind of thing had not happened since the riot of 1919, and that had been done with malicious intent. Those times were over, but segregation and racial fears were still very much in vogue. So the police had them all arrested immediately after their meeting with the Panthers and taken to Fillmore District Police Station for questioning. "What are you white guys doing in dis neighborhood?" the police asked. They were uncooperative—"It's not yah business, cops!" they answered. They were politicizing the youth of their community, the same way the Panthers were doing. They visited pool halls, parks and street corners, talking to young people about the need for revolution and about class solidarity across racial and ethnic dividing lines.[27]

"We're *RISING UP ANGRY*, and we're not 'underground.' We're straight on, we're about hard, low-down-dirty, straight-on Chicago, and what we're gonna have to do to take it back and make it ours! Do it because people got to be free. So we're gonna be free, and when we see who tries to stop us, then we're gonna have to fight. All Power to the People!"–from Rising Up Angry, Volume 1, Number 1.

Rising Up Angry, the Young Patriots and the Young Lords, the group formed as a gang at first, then redirected to save their community from displacement by gentrification, all took their lead from the Illinois Black Panther Party.[28] They all talked the same talk in their understanding of the streets of Chicago and in their radical politics. Yet, before the Panther Party brought them together, there had been nothing like them in Chicago history. Chicago had been too thoroughly segregated since the race riot of 1919. The Communist Party had had people working together across segregated neighborhoods in the 1930s, but within one integrated political party. The Panthers reasoned, from Malcolm X, that first the black community had to be self-run, then Chicago could proceed toward integration. So they organized as an all-black political party that would have the black masses running the black community, while other radicals organized their own [sic] communities.

Chicago, in the spring of 1969, was experiencing the birth of a multi-ethnic, multi-class, youth rebellion under the leadership of the Illinois Black Panther Party. The Illinois Panthers, in their attempt to bring the Students for a Democratic Society (SDS) into their youthful coalition, faced a wider cultural gap, and the philosophical stances of SDS were at odds with the Panthers'. Part of the problem with SDS was the guilt the so-called "haves" take on toward the "have-nots" and their own lack of sincerity–and the street response to that guilt. "Yeah, we said we would raise some 'bread' for you guys, but we didn't mean for sure…," the SDSers would say. The Panthers' response was first to threaten to "kick their asses," and the next time to do it.[29] That beating the Panthers administered gave the insincere SDSers a reason to quit the struggle. It also let them know the character of the Illinois Panther Party. Those students who were serious learned to be blunt and aggressive, and hardworking.[30]

A faction of SDS students, calling themselves the Weathermen, who were frustrated with the everyday politicizing and wanted more immediate results, planned to storm downtown Chicago and bring on revolution. The Deputy Chairman of the Illinois Panthers advised they dump that plan and educate the people. Their leader, Mark Rudd, responded that he doubted the Panthers were serious revolutionaries. Deputy Chairman Hampton decided to educate him as to how serious he was and punched Rudd in the face.[31] The Panthers believed that violence was a valid means of educating people.

Hampton called the Weathermen faction of SDS, "Custeristic" in reference to General Custer at the Little Bighorn, as the Weathermen ran wild through downtown Chicago, breaking windows and trashing the streets.[32] Needless to say, no revolution followed their actions, and most of these rioters were arrested, jailed, sentenced and imprisoned.

Radical politics, to the Panthers, was hard work. Running the coalition was hard work and sincerity. Their methods did not exclude violence, but was not violence for its own sake. Their motivation was the dream and the promise of a raceless, egalitarian society after the revolution. The Panthers did not for a moment think they were anything but devout revolutionaries. Hampton, in particular, was impressive in his sincerity. He would use whatever it took to bring about revolution.[33] He was not strictly a warrior. He recognized that charm and restraint worked well with older, wealthy donors, and that boldness and courage worked with the young and tough. Sincerity was his bottom line, but warmth worked, and Hampton used it. "Ché!" he said to the Deputy Minister of Education, Billy Brooks. "Why you got to wear that look? Here we are trying to win people over, and you got that [hard] look!"[34] Hampton probably recognized that the Illinois Panther Party was itself a coalition, involving people from a variety of backgrounds within the black community, middle-class, poor, college graduates, doctors' sons and daughters, ex-convicts, war veterans, reformed drug dealers, and more. If they could handle that coalition, he may have thought, they could also align across race. The Illinois Panthers received criticism for involving white people in their movement, but they followed Marx, Mao, and Huey P. Newton's lead, and most of them believed in it. They determined that could work with anybody–except the police. The police they could provoke into acting like the enemy of the people that they believed them to be.[35]

The Illinois Panther Party's core membership, perhaps thirty or so members, worked sixteen hours or more a day, seven days a week. Over the time period from the office's opening in September 1968 through 1974, when the office and the Panthers shut down, the time commitment blossomed to these long hours, without pay. They worked, ate and slept with the Panther Party's 10-Point Program on their minds, and how to take the program to the people, and serve the people with it. Holding jobs became too time-consuming. Often, outside interests melted away. Evermore, the Panthers relied on their ability to get donations.[36] Illinois Deputy Minister of Defense, Bobby Rush, later estimated that the Illinois Panther Party took in about $1,000 a day (The financial records they kept were destroyed by police and FBI, or lost.). Rush estimated that about 60 percent of this money was used to fund their Free Breakfasts for Children Program or the People's Free Medical Clinic. The remainder of the money went on rent, food and utilities.[37]

The Party members also relied more and more on each other for their emotional needs. Very close friendships developed between them. Several couples were married in the Party (naturally, their being revolutionaries meant they did not use the city license bureau but had either Hampton marry them, or proclaimed they were married). They were, in the first two years, a tight-knit core group, which had its rewards and its drawbacks.

70

The feeling of camaraderie was a positive feeling, but it also could isolate Party members from outsiders, and, once they ascertained that at least one of this core group was an FBI informant, that knowledge had all the much more withering effect on their mutual trust.[38]

PANTHERS SERVE THE PEOPLE, AND THE GENDER ISSUE

As the spring of 1969 began, the Illinois Panther Party was still increasing in size and effectiveness. Its members recall it being several hundred to one thousand strong and active across the poor ghetto, spreading into the middle and working-class, black and Latino neighborhoods.[39] Its growth had been explosive in the immediate neighborhood of Miles Square.

Women were a valuable part of this growth. For instance, Joan Gray and Stephanie Grant were very personable, charming, serious, no-nonsense women, able to relate in middle-class or poor settings. They were part of a core of dedicated young women. In addition, Lynn French, a doctor's daughter, was articulate and mentally tough. It was Lynn French's responsibility to make sure distribution of the *Black Panther Community News* from the airport to its several distribution centers happened. French had been a SNCC activist until "it played out." Why was she a Panther? In her own words, "She did not accept the limitations of class, race and gender" which society put on people. She maintains that she was not forced to defer to men in the Illinois Panther Party. Nor was there sexual harassment. French explains. "Not in Chicago. We (women) would not accept it."[40]

A look at several other women in the Illinois Black Panther Party tends to bear that assertion out. Young, hard Yvonne King had a commanding presence whenever she entered a room. Joan McCarty was positive, determined and not one to bite her tongue. Brenda Harris was known for her spirit and her mouth, as were Deirdre Prince, Stephanie Grant, and Joan Gray. It is simply not possible to imagine these women putting up with abuse or deferring to anyone.

As for the other Party members, there seems to have been an element of male chauvinism reflecting the society, which the Panthers had attempted to root out, using Mao Tse-tung's writings as a guide.[41] Certainly, the issue of gender roles was present. JoNina Abron of the Detroit Panther Party relates how she learned to say "mothafuckah" like the men and put on the "necessary macho image," while Achmed Rahmad of the Illinois Chapter remembers that it was in the Illinois Panther Party where he "first took orders from a woman who wasn't my mother."[42] And taking orders in the Panther Party meant one carried them out or suffered physical consequences. The officer of the day was there to assure that those responsible accomplished what they were responsible for. Failure to do so meant physical punishment.[43]

The Party headquarters on Madison Street at Western Avenue was also an educational center for elementary radical politics, taught straight from Mao's *Red Book*, and Huey P. Newton's *Seize the Time*, and a heavy dose of the *Black Panther Community News*. Although they said they were Marxists in 1969, it appears that Marxism did not work with them except in a vague sense. It was too coldly analytic, too scientific and carried some connotations they could not accept. The idea that they were members of the Lumpen proletariat was a problem. "Lumpen" sounded too much like lump, and they felt they did not want to be called lumps of anything. Within two years, the Panthers would redefine themselves as intercommunalists, a term coined by Huey Newton.[44] Scientific socialism did not mix with a religious bent that was so much a part of the black community. The basic message of Marxism made sense, however. They understood dialectics and materialism. The idea, as they understood it, was to expose the inequitable economic base of the system in order to undermine and destroy that racist system, which, they believed, was racist because it was capitalist.

Fundamental to their actions was the philosophical base that Malcolm X had created and under which they worked: Respect black people (or "self" as the Muslims put it), serve the people, take control of your community first, from those who controlled it (worry about integration later),[45] and align with other revolutionary youth doing the same thing, in their communities. The ultimate goal was to bring about the end of competition and unbridled individualism and create communities of cooperative economics and shared wealth. The Party theoretician, Huey Newton, called this intercommunalism.[46]

Fundamental for the Panthers was their program, rather than any individual leader. They themselves had no formal leader. Following Chinese Communism, they followed the mass line: the needs of the masses were to be heard, with solutions offered by the Party and effected by the masses and the needs of the masses were met. Individualism was dangerous and selfish. Liberalism was ineffective; talk, sympathy, but no achievable act. Mass action was democratic and therefore most fair.[47]

They wanted to sell the people of their community on that program, not on a leader. They believed they were carrying out a program that would change people's lives. They believed in the people's leadership and were excited with their perceived potential for genuine revolution. The Panthers believed they could bring the people's revolutionary potential alive by getting the people to believe in themselves, through first serving, and then educating the people. The people are tough enough to do anything, they said,[48] simply make believers of them. Serve the people. Prove your sincerity through your acts, and the people will follow your lead.

Serving the people to win the right to lead them was their motive when, in April 1969, their first Free Breakfast for Children program opened at the Better Boys Foundation on Pulaski Avenue near 16th Street. The Better Boys Foundation had resisted them, had not wanted a revolutionary program in their midst. However, the Illinois Panthers, largely local boys, used persuasion and threats to get this agency, run by outsiders to their community (a typically colonial situation), to respond positively to them.[49]

If the Better Boys Foundation wanted to be a part of their community, it needed to cooperate. Free breakfast for children was an idea from the Oakland Panther headquarters, based on a survey of the black community there, but the need for warm breakfasts for Chicago children was apparently just as real. The Panthers stated, we, the young adults in our community, will find a way to feed our own.[50] Having enough to eat, the Panthers said, was a right every American child should have. The program was a success.

The Illinois Panthers then searched high and low for more community centers willing to allow them the chance to feed local children. Not surprisingly, the local Protestant churches, many of them beholden to the Democratic Party, uniformly turned them down. Some Catholic churches, on the other hand, welcomed the Panther free breakfast programs. For example, the white priests at St. Dominic's, in the Cabrini-Green Housing Project, allowed the Panthers the use of their church for movies, forums and rallies as well. These Catholic priests responded to the idea of kids getting food and young adults serving children, ignoring the politics.[51]

When the Illinois Panthers sought food donations, however, it was the local black businessmen who most often responded. These were the same businessmen they labeled in classes as "pork-chop capitalists."

Children at a Panther-run breakfast site often drank Joe Louis milk and ate Parker House sausages.[52] Both were black-owned companies. Two members of the Party also worked for Oscar Meyer, where the black foreman gave them surplus meat.[53] The Panther free breakfast program did something for the community that no government program could: it gave the people in the community a release from the attitude that they were government dependents and gave community businessmen the opportunity to support this attitude.

By the end of May 1969, the Chicago Panthers had expanded their program to six more sites on the West and South Sides. They were feeding breakfast to approximately 4,000 children daily–while having them recite joyously, "Power to the people! Free Huey!"[54] The Panthers accomplished this without a penny of government money. Robert Lucas, local leader of a neighborhood organization on the South Side, commended them in the face of being asked to denounce them by the FBI.[55] Free Breakfast for Children program lasted as long as the Illinois Panther Party–six years.

The Panthers' effect on the children they served was probably quite powerful. To see their older brothers and sisters serving them probably made the children feel like they were something special. In a society where the self-esteem of poor children is attacked by the conditions under which they grow up, this was a unique and noteworthy accomplishment. Two of their other service programs outlived the Party–Free Busing to Prisons (for family visits) and free medical care.[56] Propagandizing people was a step they took as they served the people.

The political education classes at Panther Headquarters, every Wednesday and Friday night, required homework. They required that community volunteers and Panther members read the *Autobiography of Malcolm X*, *The Wretched of the Earth* by Franz Fanon and the *Quotations of Mao Tse-tung*, and participate in discussions. If they agreed with what they heard and continued to come to classes, they might be asked to join the Party.

Although there were monographs on Chicago that could have helped the Panthers, they did not require these works. For instance, Ovid DeMaris's *Captive City* (1968), which detailed much of how city politics worked, would have been helpful, and came out that year. The national organization had them relating to international writers, but nothing about home. In Chicago, they were on their own.

Their "gut" sense worked well in their own neighborhood, but could they learn Chicago politics before Chicago politics destroyed them and their urbanized Southern-born spirit of community? They were most assuredly handicapped for having very little knowledge of the history of the black communities on the South and West Sides.

While they were exuberantly doing so many things right, they were doing something deadly. By exuberantly advocating the violent overthrow of the United States government, they were inviting the federal government to destroy them—if it were so inclined. They were unaware of the nature of the federal government when it came to radicals, but at least one voice out of Bronzeville's past advised them against that open cry for its destruction. He was Claude "Tops" Lightfoot, former leader of the Communist Party in Chicago.[57] Claude Lightfoot had to search out the Illinois Panther Party, because they apparently had no idea Chicago had ever had radical black leaders. They were young adults of the late 60s who had grown up in an era when black Communists were disappearing. In 1969, most of the Panthers seemingly assumed they were the first revolutionary radicals the black community had ever seen.

The black Communists hoped to be able to work with them, but how did one reason with overnight success? The message Claude Lightfoot brought them was to stop advocating violence and guns.[58]

Fred Hampton in a public speech, Spring 1969:

> We gonna organize and dedicate ourselves to revolutionary
> political power and teach ourselves the specific needs of
> resisting the power structure, arm ourselves, and we're gonna
> fight reactionary pigs with INTERNATIONAL
> PROLETARIAN REVOLUTION!...We have to understand
> very clearly that there's a man in our community called a
> capitalist. Sometimes he's black, and sometimes he's white. But
> that man has to be driven out of our community, because
> anybody who comes into the community to make profit off
> the people by exploiting them can be defined as a capitalist.
> And we don't care how many programs they have, how long a
> dashiki they have. Because political power does not flow from
> the sleeve of a dashiki, political power flows from the barrel of
> a gun—it flows from the barrel of a gun.[59]

As of the Spring of 1969, the Illinois Panther Party had been an overwhelming success—if only a local one. Nevertheless, they had encountered some problems. For example, someone had tried to begin a feud between the Panthers and the P. Stone Nation. In addition, some person or persons unknown were writing hostile letters to P. Stone and the

Conservative Vice Lords, supposedly from the Panthers; and the news media were printing lies and misleading stories about them. Some places they were invited to visit were suddenly hostile to them when they arrived, and they were not sure why. However, from what has just been pointed out, one can see that success had been their immediate experience. Their successes were an explosive growth in numbers, commendations on their social service programs, and a successful coalition across poor neighborhoods in Chicago.

Black Nationalists and the Panther Party

Perhaps this section of the chapter would not be necessary but for the context of the historiography of the Black Panther Party. When lay people or historical scholars speak of the Black Panther Party, they often label them as a black nationalist organization. In fact, this appellation would insult the Panther Party members. The Black Panthers had approximately the same relationship to black nationalists as the Chinese Communists had to the Chinese Nationalists. Furthermore, the nationalists of 1968 up to the present have been cultural nationalists in the sense of their emphasis on an African culture and their belief in a Pan-African union. They have, in the wake of the Panther Party's demise, taken over the language of black activism and fitted it to their own purposes. As a result, black people are now called African Americans, and some black educators propose to be Afrocentric, while labeling white Americans as Eurocentric, and teach Kwanzaa and use Swahili in an affectation of "Africanisms." While Africans from Morocco to Mozambique are learning English, Fortran, and whatever else is useful for survival.

That emphasis on Africanisms was superfluous as far as the Black Panther Party was concerned. Panther spokesperson Fred Hampton explained in 1969:

> We don't care if niggahs wear dashikis. You understand? That's
> not gonna mean wrong time, with the wrong people…They
> say, niggah, how come your name ain't changed [but] ask the
> pigs in California who do they fear most? Ron Mamalama
> Karenga, or Huey P. Newton, who is named after a demagogic,
> lying politician, Huey P. Long. And pigs don't care about that
> in the final analysis… When they come in here with tanks, you
> come out with dashikis and nothing but dashikis…you're in
> the wrong place at the… Changing your name is not gonna
> change our set of arrangements. [If I changed my name]

> Instead of me being Fred under fascism, I'll be Ooga Booga
> under fascism... And any niggah that runs around here tellin'
> you that when your hair's long and you got a dashiki on, and
> you got bubus and all these sandals... then you're a
> revolutionary, and anybody that doesn't look like that, he's
> not–that man has to be out of his mind![60]

There was a spiritual strength in being a member of the Black Panther Party that came from its affirmation of the here and now and in simply being who they were. They adopted no affectations of African manners. They attempted to look at what they called "objective reality" and pragmatically rectified it. The Panthers embodied an attitude of self-respect and dignity for their culture, which included elements of West African culture, but which required no excess gear, nothing that did not flow from their way of life. Members of the Illinois Black Panther Party were proud of who they were, whether they were semi-literate youngsters, ex-street hustlers, or college graduates. They felt they had nothing to be ashamed of in being revolutionaries and much to be proud of–their heritage, their values of right and wrong (with its Christian base) and their dedication to the people. Being a member of the Black Panther Party was something to take pride in. They cursed, most of them did, in a city–black Chicago–where cursing was looked on as "low-class." Hampton argued, "We Marxist-Leninist niggahs, and we some Marxist-Leninist cussin' niggahs, and we gonna continue to cuss goddamnit. Cause that's what we relate to. That's what's happenin' in Babylon."[61] They did not care if middle-class Americans did not like their language. They were who they were. That was the implicit message in their language–I am who I am, accept me or don't accept me. I make no apologies.

The Panthers' attention to "objective reality" and their pragmatism in dealing with that reality were a strength. For example, they had no problem making alliances with Appalachian whites, Puerto Ricans, black gangbangers, or white college students. That the black nationalists could criticize them for that, while themselves talking of Pan-African alliances, seemed impractical to them.[62] The Panthers were more familiar with the Puerto Ricans across the street than with the Africans two thousand miles away.

Culturally, the Panthers were, for the most part, people from the West Side community, with strong Southern roots, who knew and affirmed the ways of that community–except where the people tended to accept abuse.

That idea they would not accept. And their manner of dealing with it was, as community leader Nancy Jefferson put it: "The Panthers were like the old-time folks, not afraid to get somebody told."[63] They were a Southern people, fighting Chicago's system like their ancestors fought the Klan, with a unity that comes with oppression. Their community was so totally locked out of the political system that there were few "bought-out" black leaders to betray them, or bring them into the system and allow them to work their revolution, or radicalism from within.

Their own upbringing taught these young people not to hate white people, or any ethnic group, so a Marxist class analysis worked for them, where Elijah Muhammad's racist analysis did not. When Elijah Muhammad said, the white man is the devil, he certainly inferred, and meant, it was inherently not good to work with white people.[64] In contrast, anti-racism was pragmatic. How could a minority change America without alliances? Once one accepted the idea of a revolution in America, alliances precluded a strictly racial analysis. A minority must align with others to effect the desired change. Remaking a racist world may have been naive, but it could also be seen as simply optimistic.

Basic to their optimistic spirit was their own culture, without much book-learned sophistication. Socialism sounded like sharing to them, so they accepted it. The average Party members said okay to socialism because they looked *in* a person's eyes, listened to his tone, and judged his actions in regard to what he (or she) said. They did not join the Panther Party any more than the Party joined them. That is to say, when the neighborhood Panthers accepted intellectuals like Fred Hampton and Lynn French, it was not because of their intellect, or the sophistication of their message, but because they appeared to be sincere, and they appeared to be fighters, and they thought the way the migrant Southern black already thought. They were ready for war and looking for warrior leaders. These warriors tested Fred Hampton, and Hampton proved himself on a trip to Detroit, to "straighten out" that chapter.[65]

Excluded from Chicago politics, and strongly in touch with their Southern roots, the Panthers moved with the best their community had to offer, courage and pragmatism, and with its weakness, ignorance of the society from which it had been excluded–particularly when their Party's leaders were in jail.

The black nationalists came from a more urbanized background, with more formal education. Sociologist E. Franklin Frazier described their dilemma in his study of the black middle class, *Black Bourgeoisie,* published in 1957. Having rejected their social heritage as inferior and "common" and having taken up the heart of a white, racist education, they then found themselves rejected by that white society that they had been taught to look up to. Since they regarded their black heritage as "backward," they had to fill the spiritual no-man's land they confronted with something. Dr. Frazier asserts they escaped into an unreal world of materialism, ostentatiousness and affectations.[66]

In the late 1960s, Chicago, that escapist need was still prevalent, and the cultural nationalists provided another escape, for the black middle-class, a semi-mythic African past. It was semi-mythic in that they claimed to be able to prove some rather unprovable facts (for example, Jesus Christ being black or Moses).[67] To explain the "backwardness" of black American culture, they exaggerated the effects of a cruel and brutal history, and they ignored the fact that black Americans had learned to deal with slavery and its aftermath, creatively. The nationalists believed in the "backwardness" of black American culture; the Black Panthers did not.

The black nationalists created for themselves an interest in anything African: dress, language, habits, expressions, foods. Some of this seemed to be purely for escapist purposes. For example, black Chicagoans were taught at the "Topographical Center," on 75th and St. Lawrence Avenue, that drums on rooftops would signal the next black riot across the city–rather than by phones, walkie-talkies, or even flashlights.[68] They taught the proper Swahili pronunciation of words like kuji-chagalia. Children were offered courses in Egyptian hieroglyphics, and black instructors recreated "centuries-old" customs.[69]

Much of this was a positive attempt to create a healthy environment for black children in racist society; however, that does not negate the unprovable nature of the "facts" they proposed to teach. Nor did it help the contemporary black society deal with the real and immediate problems of poor housing, unemployment, drugs, police brutality. Real problems were solved in one's current reality, with tools fashioned from that society. Black Americans were, like it or not, Americans. This was home, and Afro-Americans were creators of much that the world considered American. Black Americans have been in America as long as any ethnic group–with the exception of the Native Americans.

The nationalists were ambitious, and they were believers in capitalism. They oppose us, Panther Deputy Chairman Hampton said, "because it's sort of hard to burn down on Tuesday, what you just bought on Monday."[70]

The Nationalists did not want to change the economics of the society. They simply wanted a place reserved for their economic success within it. They pushed for black businesses in the black community, or black principals in black high schools, black coaches for black teams. The Panthers, on the other hand, pushed for businesses accountable to the community, good principals in black schools, good coaches for community teams. The opposition between them could and did become bitter. And, in fact, precipitated a split within the Panther Party between its former SNCC members, led by Stokely Carmichael and the Huey P. Newton Panthers. Most of the Illinois Panthers lined up with Newton. Fred Hampton stated his rationale in 1969:

> You have a situation where every Saturday, people get up, they worry about what kind of clothes to wear, and if they can't get a new, pretty dress, then they can't go. And they come out of the meeting, and you say, 'What was the text... ?' And they say, 'I don't know, but he had on a beautiful turtleneck.' Who are they programming for? You got black Easter, you got black Christmas, you got black Groundhog Day, you got black April Fool's Day—ain't geared for nobody but black businessmen. And I say that anybody that comes into our community and sets up any type of situation that does not meet the needs of the masses, then I, Chairman Fred of the Black Panther Party, say, that I'll take that niggah by his turtleneck and beat him to death with a Black Panther newspaper! And we could kill him with the paper, because that paper has an ideology...[71]

As capitalists, the black nationalists were no threat to the economic status quo. They went about their drive for individual success. They were not conservatives, politically. The nationalists, like the Panthers, raged at the racism of America. However, their rage was the anger that they, as educated, well-behaved blacks, were *still* discriminated against. It was not the rage that would mobilize a revolution.[72] Their rage was real, but they did not focus it to attack the economic system. It was born out of accepting and believing in a hierarchical system that did not respect poor people.

Ron Karenga's United Slaves was an example of the nationalist mindset. Judging by their deeds, they, like the gangbangers, had no trouble killing black men when pushed.[73] The United Slaves (US) seemed to inhibit directing their rage at its source, those who controlled their community, however. Their actions thereby betrayed a racist, anti-black mentality. In Southern California, US killed six Panthers in the late from 1968 to 1970.[74] Potentially, the Black Panther Party could move people in a way the nationalists could not, and they were demonstrating that ability. They were, generally speaking, broke, having enough to eat but nothing left over for fashionable clothes, cars, dental or health care or even for a telephone.[75] Nevertheless, in Chicago, they ran six free breakfast for children programs, a free health clinic and a free legal assistance clinic (and later a free busing to prisons service for visitors), with no government money, relying on donations and volunteers.

With that level of idealism and anti-capitalism, it was highly probable that a revolutionary organization that verbally attacked the United States government, a revolutionary organization, anti-capitalists in fact, as well as in their dialogue, which was verbally attacking the United States government, might not live long–depending on the nature of that government. And if the revolution did not occur, the establishment could erase the heart of its message from historic memory. And the messages of the Black Panther Party were simple messages: "Don't fight white racism with black racism, fight racism with solidarity,"[76] Serve the people. The solution to racism is in political and economic revolution.[77]

The Illinois Panthers represented poor, young black people. In their positive affirmation of who they were was their key to liberation from the second-class citizen mentality. In their political brashness (and the intolerance of the establishment to that brashness) were the seeds of their destruction.

Notes

1. bell hooks, *Killing Rage: Ending Racism* (New York: Henry Holt, 1995), 29.
2. Fred Hampton, "It's a Class Struggle, Goddammit!" speech delivered at Northern Illinois University, November 1969, published in *Vita Wa Watu: A New Afrikan Theoretical Journal*, Book Eleven (August 1987).
3. Interview with Carlos Flores, former member of the Young Lords, conducted at the Third Unitarian Church of Chicago, September 1996. Flores described how the Young Lords turned toward social action, heavily influenced by and eventually aligned with the Illinois Black Panther Party.
4. "Converting a Gang into Organization Men," *Newsweek*, June 5, 1967.
5. J. David Greenstone and Paul E. Peterson, *Race and Authority in Urban Politics* (New York: Russell Sage Foundation, 1973), 22.
6. Peter Knauss, *Chicago: A One-Party State* (Urbana: University of Illinois Press, 1972), 116.
7. Interview with Phil Cohran, summer 1980. This occurrence was also mentioned in interviews with Jewel Cook and Henry English in the summer of 1981.
8. Based on the same sources cited in the previous note: Jewel Cook, Henry English, and Phil Cohran.
9. Interview with Willie Calvin and Henry English, former Illinois Black Panther Party members who participated in this mission, July 1981.
10. Interview with Marianne Jackson, attorney who defended one of the Blackstone Rangers' "Main 21," April 1994.
11. *Brief for Plaintiff-Appellants Anderson, Bell, Clark, Satchell, and Truelock*, No. 77-1698, Appeals from the United States District Court for the Northern District of Illinois, Eastern Division, 7. Plaintiffs' Exhibit No. 138, a report by FBI informant William O'Neal to Roy Mitchell of the FBI Chicago office regarding a meeting between the Blackstone Rangers and the Panthers. Hereafter cited as the *Appeals Brief*.
12. Interview with James Montgomery, attorney for Jeff Fort, conducted summer 1982. Both Montgomery and Marianne Jackson, who defended Michael Hairston of the Black P. Stone Nation, emphasized that the Stones were largely motivated by economic interests.
13. Montgomery interview. The fact that Jeff Fort served as a pallbearer at Fred Hampton's funeral also supports this interpretation.
14. John Fish, *Black Power/White Control: The Struggle of the Woodlawn Organization in Chicago* (Princeton: Princeton University Press, 1973), 31.
15. Fish, *Black Power/White Control*, 140–149.
16. Fish, *Black Power/White Control*, 168.
17. *Chicago Tribune*, December 22–26, 1967.

18. Clifford Kelley, former alderman and radio talk show host, broadcast on WVON 1390, September 1995.

19. Interview with Deborah Johnson (Akua Njeri), Hampton's fiancée, September 1982.

20. Author's observation based on interviews conducted between 1982 and 1984 with former members of the organization. Many remained deeply committed to the ideals of the movement and expressed disappointment in the failure of the revolution they had attempted. Only two of the twenty individuals interviewed had returned to the street activities from which the Party had previously drawn them.

21. Author's recollection of meeting Joan Gray, Stephanie Grant, and Yvonne King while working as a twenty-two-year-old schoolteacher. All were avid readers, particularly when reading related to problems they sought to solve. When Fred Hampton was killed, books found in his bedroom reportedly included a guide on delivering babies—his fiancée was eight months pregnant—and a book on persuading others.

22. The Fred Hampton Law School operated for approximately five years at 45th Street and Drexel Avenue, on the northeast corner of the intersection in Chicago.

23. The Muntu Dance Theatre.

24. Interview with Lynn French, Washington, DC, April 1994.

25. Michael Gray, *American Revolution II* (film). The Chicago Public Library film collection at the Harold Washington Library Center contains this documentary, which records Bobby Lee's work as an Illinois Panther with residents of Uptown and with the Young Patriots.

26. Interview with Rev. John Auer, United Methodist Church of Rogers Park, who hosted the Young Patriots' Free Breakfast Program, July 12, 1985.

27. Interview with Mike James, founder of *Rising Up Angry*, conducted at the Heartland Café in Rogers Park, Chicago, April 11, 1996.

28. There was also a splinter group of Students for a Democratic Society (SDS), the People's Survival Committee, which maintained an office on Halsted Street south of Webster. Another group, the National Committee to Combat Fascism, operated at 35th Street and Indiana Avenue; both organizations were associated with the Panthers.

29. Cook, Calvin, and Brooks interview.

30. Interview with Flint Taylor, former member of SDS and later attorney with the People's Law Office, July 1995.

31. Flint Taylor interview.

32. Cook, Calvin, and Brooks interview.

33. Michael Gray and Howard Alk, *The Murder of Fred Hampton* (film). Harold Washington Library Center Media Collection, Chicago. In the film

Hampton leads the Panthers and their allies in repeating the statement: "I am a revolutionary! I am willing to die for the international proletarian revolutionary struggle."

34. Interview with former Panthers Jewel Cook and Cleveland Cook.

35. G. Louis Heath, *Off the Pigs! The History and Literature of the Black Panther Party* (Metuchen, NJ: Scarecrow Press, 1976), 30.

36. Interview with Yvonne King, former deputy minister of labor, Illinois Black Panther Party, July 1983.

37. Interview with Bobby Rush, founder and former minister of defense of the Illinois Black Panther Party, Chicago, April 2, 1983.

38. Interview with Joan Gray, former Panther, Chicago, October 21, 1996.

39. Rush interview.

40. French interview.

41. David Hilliard, *This Side of Glory: The Autobiography of David Hilliard and the Story of the Black Panther Party* (Boston: Little, Brown, 1993), 12.

42. Interviews with JoNina Abron and Ahmad Rahman, former Panthers, conducted at the Organization of American Historians (OAH) meeting in Chicago, 1996.

43. King interview.

44. Huey P. Newton, *To Die for the People* (New York: Random House, 1972), 31–33. Newton explains how the Black Panther Party moved from nationalism toward Marxism and eventually toward what he termed "intercommunalism."

45. George Breitman, ed., *Malcolm X Speaks: Selected Speeches and Statements* (New York: Merit Publishers, 1965), 22.

46. Newton, *To Die for the People*, 39–43.

47. Huey P. Newton, "A War Against the Panthers: A Study of Repression in America," PhD diss., University of California, Santa Cruz, 1980, 36–37.

48. Akua Njeri, *My Life with the Black Panther Party* (Chicago: Burning Spear Publications, 1991), 11–14. Njeri was formerly known as Deborah Johnson, fiancée of Fred Hampton and a member of the Illinois Black Panther Party.

49. Interviews with Billy Brooks, Willie Calvin, Jewel Cook, and Henry English. See also interview with Eugene Perkins, former director of the Better Boys Foundation, conducted at the Better Boys Foundation, September 1982.

50. Newton, "A War Against the Panthers," 38.

51. Interview with Father Paul, St. Dominic Church, Cabrini-Green Housing Project, Chicago, spring 1982.

52. Brooks, Cook, and Calvin interviews.

53. Interview with Cleveland Cook and Jewel Cook, spring 1982.

54. The practice of leading children in songs during the Free Breakfast Program is documented in the film *The Murder of Fred Hampton*, directed by Michael

Gray. Locations of the breakfast programs were identified by former Panthers Deborah Johnson (Akua Njeri), Billy Brooks, Gregory Garrett, and Yvonne King.

55. Interview with Robert Lucas, former president of the Congress of Racial Equality (CORE) and director of the Kenwood–Oakland Community Organization (KOCO), June 1985.

56. Interviews with Joan McCarty and Gregory Garrett, former Panthers who continued operating the Free Busing Program after the Panthers disbanded in 1974. Garrett interview, Chicago, June 1978; McCarty interview, Atlanta, Georgia, summer 1995.

57. Claude Lightfoot Papers, DuSable Museum of African American History, Chicago.

58. Lightfoot Papers.

59. Fred Hampton, speech published in *Vita Wa Watu: A New Afrikan Theoretical Journal*, 87.

60. Hampton, *Vita Wa Watu*, 23.

61. Philip S. Foner, ed., *The Black Panthers Speak* (Philadelphia: J. B. Lippincott, 1970), 79.

62. Huey P. Newton, *To Die for the People* (New York: Random House, 1972), 45–49.

63. Interview with Nancy Jefferson, director of the Midwest Community Council, June 1981.

64. Aminah Beverly McCloud, *African American Islam* (New York: Routledge, 1995), 29.

65. Interview with Jewel Cook, September 1981.

66. E. Franklin Frazier, *Black Bourgeoisie* (New York: Free Press, 1957), 123–129.

67. For example, see Walter A. McCray, *The Black Presence in the Bible: Discovering the Black and African Identity of Biblical Persons and Nations* (Chicago: Black Light Fellowship, 1995).

68. The author visited this center several times as a young man. Much of what he encountered there had a mystical quality that seemed to defy common sense.

69. Jon Rice, "A Black Institution," *Chicago Defender*, December 23, 1981, 4.

70. Fred Hampton, speech published in *Vita Wa Watu: A New Afrikan Theoretical Journal*, 11.

71. *Vita Wa Watu: A New Afrikan Theoretical Journal*, Book Eleven, 23.

72. bell hooks, *Killing Rage: Ending Racism* (New York: Henry Holt, 1995), 26–29. hooks writes that "the black rage that white power wants to suppress is not the narcissistic whine of the black privileged classes; it is the rage of the downtrodden and oppressed that could be mobilized to mount militant

resistance to white supremacy."

73. Frank Donner, *Protectors of Privilege: Red Squads and Police Repression in Urban America* (Berkeley: University of California Press, 1990), 256. Members of Ron Karenga's US Organization killed at least three Panthers in Los Angeles, including Alprentice "Bunchy" Carter and John Huggins, after being encouraged by the FBI and armed through contacts with the Los Angeles Police Department.

74. Kenneth O'Reilly, *Racial Matters: The FBI's Secret File on Black America, 1960–1972* (New York: Free Press, 1989), 309.

75. Author's recollection. As a young schoolteacher in 1969, the author spoke with several Panthers about their futures. Many expressed the belief that they would not live long and therefore were unconcerned about conventional ambitions such as owning a new car or addressing personal needs like dental care.

76. Hampton, *Vita Wa Watu*, 4.

77. Newton, *To Die for the People*, 192–193.

Chapter 5

Law Enforcement and the Illinois Black Panther Party

The initial reason for the Black Panther Party for Self-Defense, as it was first named in Oakland in 1966, was to protect the black community from police brutality. The method was confrontational. Huey P. Newton said he would confront the police with his gun in one hand and a lawbook in the other. He was true to his word.[1] His Panther Party learned the law and made use of guns in confronting the police. Newton, by his actions, whether he realized it or not, was making a statement to the rest of America about police that said: watch the police, because they will fail to respect the law in order to destroy us. They are not protectors of the law themselves. They are protectors of their own authority. They will demand submission without respecting us. Deputy Chairman Fred Hampton of the Illinois Panthers added, "and Oakland [Panthers] never had to deal with the likes of Chicago police."[2]

The relationship between the Chicago Police Department and the black community would prove to be the most sensitive issue upon which an atmosphere of revolution could be created. This chapter will explore why and how.

In 1966, at the age of twenty-two, Howard Saffold became a Chicago police officer. One of his first experiences on the beat, one that was most important to him, occurred that fall of 1966.[3] He and his partner, a ten-year veteran, were chasing a speeding auto down Sacramento Avenue. The red convertible they were chasing darted in and around traffic, through a red light at Fullerton Avenue, heading south at 60 m.p.h., with the police right behind it. The three kids in the car were Puerto Ricans. The car swerved to avoid a collision, skidded up on the sidewalk, and got stuck between a hydrant and a "mercado."

The three boys tumbled out, and two escaped. The last of the three kids, the driver, was too slow. The veteran officer caught him, slammed him into the narrow gangway between two stores. The big veteran, about six feet, two hundred twenty pounds, took his night stick and plunged it into the skinny kid's stomach. He turned his head, yelling back to Howard, "Heh, Howie, call for back up!" Howard did not see the need, but he called anyway, while his partner got in two more hits. Two minutes later, another squad car arrived. The veteran invited the two officers to join him. One officer knocked a tooth loose with his gloved fist, and the other crashed a blow into the kid's ribs. By that time, the scene had spectators shouting for them to stop it. It might as well have been a cheering section. "C'mon, Howie, get your licks in!" Saffold's partner urged.

Saffold was a little shaken. "No, you guys handled it." His partner noted the look on Saffold's face as they threw the kid into the wagon. "Look, Howie," he said, "this cocksucker here is gonna have a white shirt, a tie, a priest and a mother when he goes before the judge. He's gonna get his wrist slapped, maybe. This way we teach them up front, ya see?" Saffold saw all right, but it made him wonder, because his partner was not a bad guy. Officer Saffold did not quit the police department in disgust. He learned from it, and he kept his pride as a police officer.[4] Certainly, the Chicago Police Department, from the dozen officers I have interviewed, eleven black, one white, was something they all took pride in. This fact would not have been so if they felt this police department was itself immoral. However, the particular incident described above shows the considerable degree of freedom police officers had at their disposal when making an arrest. It also indicated the potentially dangerous situation of police officers and their manner of dealing with the dangers of the job. Finally, it gave the hint that some police believed they not only represented the law, but that they *were* the law. So what did the rougher cops do if the good police so casually accepted this type of behavior?

Some Characteristics of Police in the 1960s

In a one-year analysis of the Chicago Police Department, conducted by the Chicago Law Enforcement Study Group in 1972, they noted that the Chicago Police Department (CPD) consistently resisted civilian review of police misconduct, and that the police practically never found a fellow police officer guilty of anything, except a minor misconduct.[5] This conclusion echoed a similar conclusion of the American Civil Liberties Union (ACLU) report published in 1966.[6] The police across America are a fraternity that protects their own, according to Jerome Skolnick and Elliot Currie and other sociologists. Police officers themselves often referred to their fraternal nature. In a survey of New York City Patrolmen, two-thirds agreed that "a police department is really a large brotherhood in which each patrolman does his best to help all other patrolmen."[7] The report in which this survey was included, from *The Police Community, Dimensions of an Occupational Subculture* (New York, 1975), goes on to state, "police corruption results from this solidarity and their animosity toward the public. It is a 'nobody likes us, so the hell with them' attitude.'" This attitude, the report adds, is particularly true of white cops in black ghettoes. Other sociological studies support that assertion.[8] Reasonably, the degree of alienation would probably influence the extent to which police would go to protect one of their own. Sufficiently pushed, it stands to reason that the police would back up their fraternity "brothers" no matter what they had done.

In the 1960s, all across America, the tensions between black communities and the police were growing. As the urban ghettoes became more politically aware and the people in them more discontented with the overt racism of their segregated communities, run by outsiders, the police were the most directly affected, although they had not created the conditions there. As one policeman argued, "If there are social injustices, that's society's bag. We can't cure them. All we can do is make arrests."[9]

The police would sometimes make arrests without a crime having been committed. Here is how that worked, according to those who have studied police behavior. The most serious crime, to the average police officer, was "contempt of cop," Jerome Skolnick asserted, and several sociologists have agreed.[10] If the police did not get that respect, according to sociologist William Westley, in a study done in 1970, the police tended to provoke the citizen, and then the police would retaliate with violence.[11] Carl Werthan and Irving Piliavan in *The Police, Six Sociological Essays* also noted this phenomenon (Wiley and Sons, 1966). Once an officer abused a citizen who had not respected him, he had to charge him with something to justify the abuse. Middle-level police, sergeants and lieutenants backed up the lie, these authors say. Skolnick and Currie agree, the chief abuse of police power, they assert, is the lie that makes a quarrel look like a crime. "Once an officer has abused another citizen, he must charge him with something to justify the abuse."[12]

Finally, speaking of police in general, racism and conservatism are noted within most police departments studied. Paul Chevigny, in his book *Police Power* (Pantheon Books, 1969), describes the extent to which minor altercations between citizen drivers, or husbands and wives, were worsened by the presence and actions of police if the citizens were minorities. He found this to be the case because police entered the situation and tried to establish authority with unconditional demands, and/or the use of force. Police believed that minority people who fear them, or show fear of them, will obey them, and so they try to induce fear through aggressive behavior.[13] The weakness in this type of challenge is that it is most acceptable to the citizen who fears being caught at a crime he (or she) is in the act of committing, and is least acceptable to a citizen who feels he or she is doing something right, or, as in the case of the Panthers, something noble. Phillip Westley, in his study of a Midwest police department, as well as Werthman and Piliavin, assert that the police tended to be very aggressive with minorities and even had a tendency to provoke anyone disrespectful, until there was an assault, and then they would retaliate.[14]

The police interviewed in a New York survey of 1966 would maintain, almost in every case of questionable arrest, that they had to preserve their authority against those who challenged it, in order to enforce the laws effectively.[15] In short, their authority over others would be lost if they backed down from a single person. It followed that an officer's authority was asserted in situations that were personal disputes. In some of these cases, the provocation came from the citizen, and in some it came from the officer; however, the point is that there were arguments like everyday citizens have, but they involved an officer. For that officer, no argument was purely personal but a challenge of his authority.[16] So the police were already prone to act in a certain way if provoked, and were conditioned to act in an even more authoritative fashion in a nonwhite community.

CHARACTERISTICS OF THE CHICAGO POLICE DEPARTMENT IN THE BLACK COMMUNITY

The primary abuses of Chicago police in the black community, as reported in the *Chicago Defender* in 1956, had been disrespect of citizens, torturing of suspects, arbitrary arrests and failure to arrest certain persons.[17] However, in the next ten years, relations between cops and blacks had worsened. The civil disobedience of the Chicago Freedom Movement had polarized the Chicago Police Department, particularly around the issue of housing open to all races. Many patrolmen, being white residents of the very neighborhoods the open-housing marchers targeted for protest marches, found the issue of integration a threat to their neighborhood, as did their neighbors. Black activists were their enemies because these police, like their neighbors, believed the presence of black residents would harm their communities. Some officers quit rather than protect the demonstrators. Other officers did the job of protecting marchers very reluctantly.[18] Here was the basis for the increased alienation between Chicago police and Chicago's black citizens.

In Chicago, a political factor negatively affected the black community. Chicago, in 1969, [as much as Moscow that same year] had a one-party political system. Consequently, when the police department was answerable to City Hall, it was also answerable to the Cook County Democratic Party. There were officers in the police department who advanced faster and further because they were willing to carry out political favors for the Democratic Party.[19] In the past, these favors had included political assassinations, as we have seen. Black political activists were also well aware of this factor. It was in this atmosphere that the Panther Party felt impelled to be provocative. In a manner of speaking, that provocation may have been a way of telling the police that they were not intimidated by the threat of assassination.

In 1967, city alderman Thomas Keane, one of Mayor Daley's closest associates, said what Chicago needed was more police to deal with the likes of Dr. Martin Luther King Jr., who, though nonviolent himself, was a front for violence.[20] Following this speech on the floor of the city council, seven hundred new police officer positions were created in 1968. One can logically conclude that the majority of people taking these positions, in those times of social turmoil, were not much in sympathy with black activists nor ghetto residents in general. Attitude surveys of police, taken in the late sixties, bear this out. Jerome Skolnick's *The Politics of Protest*, for example, points out that in the opinion of most police, the people who lived there created the conditions of the black ghetto—despite considerable evidence to the contrary—and the civil rights movement was Communist.[21]

As if all these factors were not enough to make violence between police and Panthers probable, there is one more significant factor when studying the Chicago police and the black community of the late 1960s. There was a white officer on the Chicago Police Department who patrolled North Lawndale, who was a card-carrying member of the Ku Klux Klan (by his own admission). In fact, he drove to work with KKK spray-painted on the trunk of his car.[22] Rumor was that he carried a night stick, hollowed out, with a lead pipe shoved up inside it, and that they had punished him for beating a white kid senseless with it, by assigning him to the black West Side, at the Fillmore District Station. Apparently, this "punishment" was standard procedure.[23] Although the West Side ghetto needed more sensitive policing, it got more of the brutal, racist police. What distinguished this patrolman from fifty other Ku Kluxers on the force (according to the Klan),[24] was that the media "discovered" his membership in the KKK (he was not hiding it), and he and five other klansmen were expelled from the department. What did they say their role was as Klansmen in the CPD? They were there to let black people know there were police willing to keep them in line. The situation in Chicago was heavily weighted in favor of more violence between police and black activists and a worsening community/cop relationship.

The Police Fraternity

In the spring riot of April 1968, the black ghetto's response to Dr. King's assassination, the police were credited with doing a good job of containing an uprising of angry citizens. They used a minimum of deadly force and were praised for their restraint and regard for lives. They displeased Mayor Daley, on the other hand, and he issued his much-publicized "shoot to kill arsonists, shoot to maim looters!" orders.[25] Soon after, Chicago police began to patrol the black communities armed with loaded shotguns. The consequences of the Mayor's attitude and resulting actions were, according to independent investigators, "unmistakable and irrevocable."[26] His words unleashed the more violent of the police force. In the Democratic Party's national convention that followed that summer, restraint was almost nonexistent. As radical hippies, liberals and innocent passersby were beaten by police in the streets of downtown Chicago, the Illinois Panther Party was forming, three miles due west.

The spring of 1969 began where the violence of the summer of 1968 ended. The more extreme cases involved deaths, and these were the very cases with which the Black Panther Party involved itself. On May 1, 1969, for example, Charles Cox, black, age twenty, was found dead in a cell at the Fillmore District Station. A private pathologist testified in court that Cox died of blows to his head. Cox, of 3924 W. Monroe (West Garfield), had been arrested the night before. He and his friend were either causing a disturbance or walking down the street, disturbing no one, depending on whom you believe, when the police picked them up. Cox was held, and his friend was released. He returned with more friends, insisting Cox be released. He was told no one named Charles Cox was there, yet he claimed he heard his friend's voice. Cox definitely *was* there, and the next morning his body was prepared for burial. The police listed a drug overdose as the cause of death, but the skull evidenced a severe beating.[27]

One week later, May 8, another killing by police was making the news. This time, the victim was 35-year-old M.C. Green of Trumball Street. On that same day, another complaint came to black State Senator Charles Chew, from a youth beaten by a white mob, then taken by police and beaten again.[28]

On May 13, a West Side rally protested the killing of another teen, 17-year-old James Johnson. Johnson and his friends had run a red light and sped away with the police in pursuit. After their car hit a post, the police caught them, and then, according to eyewitnesses, shot him dead, without provocation.[29] May turned to June, and the protests and the questionable violence continued. Then, in July, police violence hit closer to home for many Panthers.

Nineteen-year-old Linda Anderson, a cousin of a Panther, got into an argument with a friend. Ms. Anderson was evidently struggling with him in her apartment when a rookie police officer came to her door. He demanded entrance, he later said. She yelled for him to go away. He went back to his squad car, picked up his new shotgun, returned and blew a hole in the door—to force his way in, he said. The shot missed the lock, he claimed he was shooting at, by a foot. It did, however, hit Linda Anderson in the face, killing her.[30]

The neighbors claimed he went to the door without knocking and shot at the woman's voice. The fact that he "missed" the lock by that much and the fact that the door was plywood and he could have kicked it in, make the officer's version the less likely of the two. The officer who killed Linda Anderson received a one-day suspension for violating police General Order 76-14, firing through a closed door. [31] The next day, scores of Panthers marched on the Fillmore Station, lining up in the street. They shouted in unison, "Death to oppressors! Off the pigs!"[32] The Police Department had made a statement by this minimal discipline on the offending officer. As the Panthers saw it, the police were willing to protect one of their own even though that one was guilty of a felony.

Two weeks later, 20-year-old Panther Larry Roberson told two Fillmore District officers involved in questioning a man about a robbery that he would not move on, because it was his right to witness an arrest. An altercation followed, and Roberson was shot in the stomach by a police officer.

Apparently recovering, Roberson was taken from a private hospital by police to the Bridewell hospital facility at Cook County Jail, where he suddenly died.[33] Roberson was the first of seven Illinois Panthers or their friends, killed under suspicious circumstances, or murdered outright by police. The others were Mark Clark, Fred Hampton, Jake Winters, John Soto, Omowale Babatunde, and Merrill Harvey.

More police violence followed. In early August 1969, a South Side youngster, Wayne Black, was killed by a police officer. The officer claimed the youth lunged at him with a knife. Three eyewitnesses denied Black had a knife. The officer went free.[34] On August 12, Maple Shorten, forty-two, in good health, was arrested by police. The next day, his wife went to the Criminal Courts Building for his hearing. They told her, "Didn't you know he's dead?"[35]

There were thirty-nine deaths of Chicagoans that year at the hands of police officers. The Illinois Panthers and their allies, the revolutionary Young Lords, marched on several police stations, held public hearings, held mock trials that indicated evidence of police misconduct, and threatened the police with violent retaliation. Not one case went to court, or even brought an indictment against police.[36]

The police violence of the years 1969 and 1970 was documented by the independent citizens' group named the Chicago Law Enforcement Study Group. And, although few Chicago police officers ever killed anyone, nevertheless, the Chicago police were four times as lethal in their enforcement of the law than New York City or Los Angeles. And, of the seventy-nine civilians killed, fifty-nine were black. In fifty-eight cases, the police said their victim had a weapon, yet in only three of those cases was a weapon found. Twenty-eight of these cases showed clear evidence of police misconduct.[37] It would not be unreasonable to assume that an organization in the police department was carrying out an agenda of control that did not rule out murder as a means.

Black Police Response

Several black police officers, concerned over the increasing violence of the police, protested that violence in 1969 by forming an organization that they named the Afro-American Patrolmen's League. They were a group of officers who put the situation in a different perspective than the average patrolman. They did not have a us-against-the-world attitude. And what made them more objective was the racism deeply embedded in the CPD.[38] Howard Saffold explained his experiences with the police intelligence unit known as the Red Squad, which "spied" on the Illinois Black Panther Party:

> Bobby Rush, age twenty-one, Chairman [Deputy Minister of Defense] of the Panthers, stepped up to the podium at the People's Church on Ashland Avenue, Near West Side. He yelled at Saffold, age 35, and his partner, "Will the pigs please leave. We ain't talkin' about nothin' until you do!" Howard Saffold and his partner looked at each other and at those around them. They were the only clean-cut, 35-40-year-olds in the group. Night after night, they were assigned to just sit there and identify those who came to the meeting. They shrugged, looked at each other again. Their eyes said, "Heh, why not?" They got up and left.

> This is intelligence work?" Saffold asked. "This is bullshit!" His partner answered. "They're not giving us intelligence work!" Back at headquarters, they wrote out their usual report: thirteen known Panthers attended such and such a meeting. Panther Robert Brown wore his usual brown leather jacket; Stephanie Grant had a red scarf sticking out of her coat pocket. Bobby Rush carried the usual satchel, as he is known to do, etc.

> Officer O'Bannion approached them, "We gunta raid da Pant'ers tomorrah!" he said. At the briefing the next morning, 200 patrolmen were assembled. The artillery and equipment were handed out and read off: Cizewski will carry a shotgun and a .357 Magnum, Officer Jones will carry a .38 and a high-beam flashlight…" Saffold and the other black cops joked to themselves about how the white boys got the heavy artillery.

> The sentiment at the station was serious and agitated. "Boy, I'd
> love to blow one of those fuckers head's off. Just one shot from
> any of them and I'm killing a motherfucker today!" one officer
> said and got several "fuckin A's!" in response.[39]

The white cops hated the Panthers, apparently for challenging their authority and calling them pigs, for disrespecting them. Yet it was similar to the disrespect they themselves showed the black community by protecting the brutal cops in their ranks who had brutalized black citizens. Now, they could have either ignored the Panthers' attitude and done their job or taken it as a challenge to their authority. The young people of the community admired the Panther attitude and enjoyed the police anger. They didn't automatically respect a person because he wore a uniform and had a gun, and they liked to challenge authority, particularly arrogant authority.

Several black officers were uneasy around what they perceived to be the racist attitude of their fellow officers. To them, the Panthers *were not* like the Nazi's, who talked about killing off Jews and blacks. In fact, the Panthers were understandable. And if they had to tolerate Ku Kluxers and Nazis in doing their job, the white cops could tolerate Panthers. One officer had grown up with a guy who had become a Panther. The guy had called him a pig, but he could see it was all rhetoric, aimed at an institution, with no personal feeling behind it. That was the way he took it.[40]

When the police burst into Panther headquarters and secured the building and one police officer got cut, they burned the building, tore out the wiring, and beat several Panthers with their guns. It was then that Officer Saffold asked to be transferred out of Police Intelligence. "Sure," they told him, "we don't want you here if you don't want to be here."[41] It seemed to him that they had not wanted him at all. They had given him a dirty job as an overt spy, a front for intimidating the Panthers, in full view of them. When his morale dipped, he got pushed out the door.[42]

Meanwhile, Saffold had gained a respect for the Panthers. Unlike gang-bangers, they did not break down under police interrogation. They did not seem to feel anyone was better than them, nor that they had been caught doing something they themselves deep down did not believe in. Police disrespect did not intimidate them. It made them angry. Saffold and many other officers admired that.[43] The Panthers, claimed one white police officer, "have invaded the police force." His accusation was probably a response to the widening gap he saw between whites and blacks within the Chicago Police Department when it came to the Black Panther Party.

Racism was so rampant within the "Red Squad," which necessarily relied on black police officers, where the Panthers were concerned, that they brought the investigation of the Panthers to a standstill.[44] The white leader of the Gang Intelligence Unit refused to accept the information he got from his black co-leader.[45] Looking through the Red Squad files, which the Chicago Police Department was forced to release to the Chicago Historical Society, it is apparent that second-hand information, such as leaflets, and any data an outsider could get, was about all the files contain. It seems apparent they could not shed their racism enough to objectively appraise the Party, nor did they want to.

According to the Grand Jury, which investigated the activities of the Red Squad from 1969 through 1972, their primary goal was not to neutralize revolutionary threats to city government but to get rid of all critics of the Daley administration. Nor did they believe it was wrong to commit burglaries, administer beatings or destroy private property to do this job.[46]

The rationale that produced a split in the conspiracy of silence among police was the racism of the police, as a whole, when it came to the Black Panther Party. Certain black officers took a stand not to go along with the brutality of their fellow officers toward black youth generally and Black Panthers in particular.

These officers founded the Afro-American Patrolmen's League and broke the fraternity of silence when it came to racial brutality. It was a move that cost them in promotions, threats and harassment. Renault Robinson, an exemplary police officer before helping to found this organization, could do nothing right after. They consistently reprimanded and harassed him, and eventually gave him a beat that was the alley behind downtown police headquarters.

Robinson and several fellow black officers filed a racial discrimination suit against the Chicago Police Department and won a multimillion-dollar settlement.[47] More germane to this story, for once, a police officer who wanted to be brutal was now having to look over his shoulder and decide whether or not his fellow officer would report him. Indirectly, it was the Panther Party's courageous stance against the police that made this check on police brutality happen. Officially, the Panthers saw all police as "pigs"–as enemies. In reality, however, they noted the difference between police officers. Black officer "Gloves" Davis, who also brutalized them like the white racist officers, was a pig. Other black officers were potentially their allies, and they recognized that. As with black businessmen who supplied them with food for their free breakfast program, they accepted that reality.

POLICE PROVOKED BY PANTHERS AND POLICE PROVOCATION

The phone rang at the new Panther headquarters on Madison and Western in the late summer of 1968. Several Panthers quit talking so that Fred Hampton could hear. "This is the Chicago Police Department." The voice said. "We've just been over to SDS and beat their door down. You cocksuckers are next!" Hampton replied, "Come on!"

That was their first encounter with the police—and they found that SDS *had* been raided.[48] By the spring of 1969, the police had made ninety-five arrests of Panther Party members. There was a pattern to these arrests: Usually, the Party member was charged with disorderly conduct and forced to pay bail to get out. Later, the charge would be dropped.[49] The tactic was successful in depleting the Panther Party's funds but, for most Panthers, it increased their spirit of determination.

A Panther's day, as has already been shown, was a busy one. Police harassment quickly became a part of this daily routine. The police might show up at the breakfast program and take photos of the children, or they might stop a volunteer, put him or her in their car, and drive them across town, then drop that volunteer off in a strange neighborhood. Some Party members were picked up and told to quit the Panther Party.[50] Party members who drove needed to drive perfectly and have nothing lacking on their vehicle, or police would stop them and ticket or arrest them.[51]

Meanwhile, at rallies, the police were not above getting thugs to attack the Panthers or their allies. For instance, a rally in virtually all-white Lincoln Park turned into a free-for-all between the Panthers and a group of black thugs. At all previous rallies, the police had been everywhere, taking photos, copying down license plate numbers. At this rally, however, they were nowhere to be found.[52]

Harassment of the free breakfast program by police was a good way for the police to lose whatever respect they had gained with the mothers and fathers of the children. Police harassment, although maddening to the Party members, aroused the local community to their support and alienated the police even further from the community. The police attitude of "we-don't-give-a-damn" was bad for them. While 1969 and 1970 were record years for citizens killed by Chicago police, 1970 was also a record year for the number of police killed by citizens (9). Former Superintendent Brzeczek attributes this statistic to the way the police went after the Panther leader, Fred Hampton.[53] It might be argued further that the way the police behaved generally with the Panther Party created a climate in which killing a police officer might be acceptable.

One of their more provocative acts that summer was to hold mock raids on Black Panther Headquarters. Two or three squad cars would come up to the door of the headquarters and pull out their guns, then return to their cars. After a few of these mock raids, they got what they wanted. The Party members inside the office shot at them.

Police provocation had pushed them to a fight. It was more serious than the police anticipated. The police evidently thought the Panthers were not going to aim at them and exposed themselves. Consequently, five police were hit by Panther fire. Then the Panthers surrendered and came out with their hands in the air.

The first one out the door got his jaw broken by a police officer swinging a rifle. The rest were forced back inside, where shots were fired over their heads. Later, taken to the station, they were forced to run a gauntlet of police with nightsticks. The smallest of them got quite excited with the severity of the beating he was receiving. He started yelling, "We musta offed a pig! We musta offed a pig!"

Meanwhile, back at the office, the police set the Panther headquarters on fire and left amidst a rain of bricks from community people, who pelted their squad cars and paddy wagons. It was July 31. 1969.[54]

The next day, people from the community came over to help the Panthers repair their office. The Panthers had become local heroes among the teenagers. They understood that type of courage. But the older people understood where it could lead. They got their kids away from the Panther Party, if they could.

The violent skirmishes between Chicago police and the Illinois Panther Party continued, confrontations neither Fred Hampton nor the Chicago Police Department wanted to continue. They ended with Hampton's murder on December 4, 1969.

However, the police were almost as badly victimized as the Panther Party. To explain how that occurred, we must look at the role of the Federal Bureau of Investigation in dealing with the Illinois Panthers.

FBI Involvement with Chicago Panthers

The Panther Party was well aware of the capabilities of the Chicago Police Department and realized that the police were often their own worst enemies in the black community. They were prepared for a battle with them and expected to win that battle for the allegiance of their community. The average cop seemed to have failed to understand he would work better in the community if he attempted to be a part of it.

When the Blackstone Rangers received a few letters, supposedly from the Panther Party leaders, the Panther leadership got on the phone and explained to the Rangers that those letters were coming from the police. It seemed to fit the police mode of operation. The letters were amateurish and yet meant to do deadly harm to the leaders of the Panthers by threatening the life of Blackstone leader Jeff Fort.[55] What the Panthers did *not* know was that the letters came from the Chicago office of the FBI. Nor did they realize that one of their own leaders was an FBI "informant," an intelligent and totally unprincipled thug by the name of William O'Neal.

In fact, the Panthers and the rest of black Chicago had no idea of the nature of the FBI's involvement in their lives. It was deadly, extralegal and racist involvement that most citizens in 1969 probably did not think was in character with the FBI. If you had asked the honest opinion of most citizens in that year, of the FBI, the great majority, black and white, would probably have said incorruptible.[35]

The FBI had not been entirely hostile to the goals of the civil rights movement. President Johnson had forced the FBI into actively breaking the back of legalized terrorism against black people in the South.[56] Disruption of the Ku Klux Klan by some two thousand FBI agents and informants in the Klan was the target, *after* the Communist Party. Hoover did, in fact, have an incorruptible bureau, answerable only to him.

Therein lay one of its weaknesses, for Hoover answered to no one, and was himself, according to two of his biographers, if not a racist, at the very least, obsessed with undermining, and if possible destroying, anyone daring to challenge the status quo.[57]

In 1963, Hoover's Assistant Director, William Sullivan, told Hoover that, after extensive research, he had found no evidence of Communist influence in the civil rights movement. Hoover challenged him, however. Hoover insisted that Communist influence must be found. Sullivan backed down, and reversed himself and was, by his own admission, later less than honest.[58] The result was the counter-intelligence program known as COINTELPRO, whose five goals were:

To prevent blacks from uniting;

To prevent the rise of a "messiah" to unify blacks;

To prevent "militant" groups from gaining respectability;

To prevent the growth of youth groups, and

To prevent violence.[59]

Except the last goal, which the FBI did not attempt to accomplish, we could view their aim as destroying the proper function of a culture. Their tactics, by Sullivan's own admission, violated the rights of American citizens. He said, "We have used [all these techniques] against the Nazi's and the Soviet agents. They have used them against us. [These same methods] were brought home against any organization against which we were targeted."[60] When it came to handling the black radicals, the FBI acted out some 379 proposals, causing deaths, serious physical, social, financial and/or psychological harm, and totally disregarding the rights of these American citizens.[61]

In Chicago, the FBI had information on a Black Panther Party a year before it existed. In an FBI memorandum dated September 8, 1967, the FBI mentioned the Black Panthers, focusing on the activities of the West Side Organization, chiefly on the editor of its newspaper, the *West Side Torch*, whose nickname was "Barracuda." He had a club called the Black Panthers, and the FBI was told he led a black nationalist organization.[62] They apparently began an investigation of him. He was a Korean War veteran, with a black belt in Judo, who had run afoul of the local Democratic Party in his attempts to curb crime in his neighborhood. "Barracuda" got involved in politics and briefly headed security at the Poor People's Campaign in Washington, D.C. in 1968. He was somehow labeled a government informant and on someone's "hit" list.

Barracuda left Chicago in 1968 and went into hiding. An attempt to find his files with the CIA produced a brief memorandum. They had something on him. They would send it. One year later, they had nothing on him.[63] His file with the FBI was lacking in solid information and inaccurate. At one point, he was described as six feet, two hundred fifty pounds, then he becomes a slender male Negro, five feet nine, one hundred sixty pounds. Inaccurate information would characterize the FBI's involvement with the Illinois Black Panther Party, largely because of with whom they chose to work, and how they chose to do it.

When the real Illinois Black Panther Party appeared in the late summer of 1968, the FBI had a "ghetto informant" ready to join the Panther Party. (The FBI, at the time, had one black agent.) Their informant was a young criminal by the name of William O'Neal, whom the police had arrested for kidnapping and beating a woman, stealing a car, and impersonating a police officer. Roy Mitchell, a local Chicago FBI agent, got O'Neal's conviction set aside on the agreement that he would join the Panthers and, ostensibly, spy on them.[64]

O'Neal was not a competent spy. His information was unreliable, often exaggerated and self-serving. What he did do effectively was cause numerous disruptions within the Illinois Panther Party and spread distrust and paranoia. He urged young Party members to commit shakedowns, committed robberies himself, tried to get the Panther Party to bomb City Hall, and constructed a torture chair to weed out "spies." He took Panthers to a rifle range for target practice, engaged in the sale of illegal drugs *with* the knowledge of the FBI, and attempted to get two of his Panther "friends" to join him in a burglary. O'Neal also whipped a Panther he labeled an informant and took explosives to a Panther fugitive in Canada. He advised Panther Jewel Cook to carry a weapon, even though it violated Cook's parole. All these activities are documented in the FBI's own files, which they were forced to turn over to the Court in the litigation against the City of Chicago and others, by the family of Fred Hampton.[65] William O'Neal's schemes to bomb and to torture were routinely turned down by the Central Staff of the Illinois Panthers, until Hampton, suspicious of him, refused to allow O'Neal to be his bodyguard. O'Neal's cadre leader, Bobby Rush, seemed neutral about O'Neal, and so he was kept in the Party until 1971.[66]

His disruptions were to include the setting up of Hampton for murder, the murder of Panther Jerry Dunigan's wife, and urging Dunigan to take revenge on innocent people he vaguely fingered–which Dunigan did. O'Neal was also involved in the hit-squad style murder of black businessmen. These escapades were financed by the FBI, which paid him at least $575 a month for two years.[67]

On January 6, 1969, the FBI arranged it so that the Chicago Police Department arrested Fred Hampton as he was about to be interviewed on local talk show radio. Not only did their timing embarrass the Panther

Party, but it prevented Hampton from reaching a wider audience. The charge against him was stealing $71 worth of ice cream from a Good Humor truck, an absurd charge for anyone who knew Hampton. It was perhaps O'Neal's only competent job as a spy (but not as an agent provocateur).

The FBI had failed in its first attempts at getting the leadership of the Panther Party "neutralized" by trying to get Black P. Stone leader Jeff Fort to kill them. They had written and mailed at least three letters to Fort, telling him, through their mythical "black man you don't know," that Hampton and Rush were out to kill him.[68] O'Neal's efforts had similarly been ineffectual at halting the sudden growth of the Party in early 1969. So, on June 5, 1969, at 5:35 a.m., the FBI raided Panther Headquarters, ostensibly looking for a fugitive from the law, one George Sams, wanted on the East Coast. Sams was actually an informant of theirs, and the Illinois Panthers *had* beaten him up. They did not know he was an informant, they related, but "we did know he was a liar," several of them later told me.[69]

The FBI used forty agents, armed with submachine guns and tear gas, and accompanied by a helicopter. The FBI called ahead, letting the Panthers know they were being raided. The Panthers quietly surrendered. FBI agents, led by Marlin Johnson, head of the Chicago Office, then took six legally purchased weapons from the Panthers, and $3,000 in donations, and a list of volunteers and a list of members, and tore out the building's wiring.[70] By Marlin Johnson's own admission, Sams had not been the purpose for the raid.

The raid accomplished what it intended. Several ex-Panthers have agreed that the community's involvement with the Black Panther Party was considerably diminished by that FBI raid. Much of their local support vanished.[71] Community people were evidently willing to do battle with Chicago politics and Chicago police, but not the federal government. The FBI had more than done its job, but perhaps would not realize it. It certainly was not in William O'Neal's interest to see that the FBI knew it had deterred large numbers of people from involving themselves with the Panthers. For him to remain important, the Panthers had to be a threat to the government. Considering his incentive (money), it was not in his own interest in relating such a consideration to the FBI. It would seem that the basic dishonesty of a man like William O'Neal, of which they already were knowledgeable, might have given the FBI pause before relying on him.

Now, the FBI, through its Chicago agent Roy Mitchell, encouraged the Chicago police Department to increase its intelligence activities. The Chicago police did just that, for its own and for the Daley administration's own political advantage, crippling several other community groups which had no revolutionary rhetoric, but were anti-Daley. The Chicago Police Red Squad's victims included the Alliance to End Repression, the Organization for a Better Austin, the Woodlawn Organization, the American Jewish Council, the Kenwood Oakland Community Organization, the Community Renewal Society, the Citizens' Action Program, and the Metropolitan Housing Alliance–all community-based organizations, as well as the Students for a Democratic Society, and more than 160 churches.[72] The police also aided and protected the illegal attacks and burglaries of a right-wing group, the Legion of Justice, as it attacked several community activist groups.[73] The Chicago Police Red Squad showed no respect for the law. The FBI had led the way, however.

O'Neal's career was garnering money, and other hoodlums may have taken the incentive from his financial success. Spying on any group and finding them revolutionary, or as O'Neal put it, "a threat," could earn an enterprising, unprincipled person considerable money.

There is no hard factual data on this, but considering the grapevine in the poor community, it is likely that people understood what O'Neal was doing. Certainly, he was discovered by police Sergeant Stanley Robinson and confessed his role as a spy.[74] Community organizing was perhaps attracting the thugs, motivating them to disrupt the process. By the summer of 1969, the Illinois Black Panther Party was no longer growing under the attacks of the FBI, the Chicago police and their paid thugs, the false charges, fictional letters, character assassinations and physical assaults, but they were persisting. They would not dissolve.

By August of 1969, they were more violence-prone. A year of provocation and the deaths of Larry Roberson and the deaths of black citizens in their community at the hands of police, who had not been punished, pushed the Illinois Panthers to a state of rage that was undermining their community support and isolating them as much as the police from their constituents.

SUMMATION

Law enforcement's effect on the Illinois Black Panther Party was, at the local level, the antithesis of its own best interests. The Chicago Police

Department showed itself to be racist and brutally so, and came under severe attack from the black community, on the street, as well as in the political arena. The police, by their brutality, generated financial support for the Panther Party, which might not otherwise have materialized. Not only did police misconduct bring support for the Party, but it also catalyzed a split in the police fraternity, with the creation of the Afro-American Patrolmen's League. This organization would suffer so much harassment at its daring to break the conspiracy of silence around police misconduct, that its leader would win a multi-million dollar lawsuit he filed against the Chicago Police Department on harassment and discrimination.[75]

The effect of the FBI's COINTELPRO was equally short-sighted and more pernicious over the long term. To quote Supreme Court Justice Brandeis in 1927:

> Our government...for good or for ill, teaches the whole people,
> by its example. Crime is contagious. If the government
> becomes a lawbreaker, it breeds contempt for law; it invites
> every man to become a law unto himself.

If there was an increase in crime in the early 1970s, the FBI had contributed mightily to it by its handling of the Illinois Black Panther Party.

Notes

1. David Hilliard, *This Side of Glory: The Autobiography of David Hilliard and the Story of the Black Panther Party* (Boston: Little, Brown, 1993), 15–78.
2. Interview with Billy Brooks, former deputy minister of education, Illinois Black Panther Party, April 12, 1995.
3. Interview with Howard Saffold, founding member of the Afro-American Patrolmen's League, July 1982.
4. Saffold interview.
5. Janice Bauer, director, *The Chicago Police Department Office of Professional Standards: A One-Year Analysis* (Chicago: Chicago Law Enforcement Study Group, 1976), 13.
6. American Civil Liberties Union, *Recommendations Regarding Administration of Civilian Complaints Against the Chicago Police Department* (New York: ACLU, July 1966).
7. Andrew Goldsmith and John Goldsmith, eds., *The Police Community: Dimensions of an Occupational Subculture* (New York: Praeger, 1975), 26.
8. Robert Wintersmith, *Police and the Black Community* (Lexington, MA: D.C. Heath, 1974), 49–55.
9. Jerome H. Skolnick, *The Politics of Protest* (New York: Clarion Books, 1969), 255.
10. Elliott Currie and Jerome H. Skolnick, *Crisis in American Institutions* (Boston: Little, Brown, 1974), 389.
11. Paul Chevigny, "Force, Arrest, and Cover Charges," in *Crisis in American Institutions*, 394.
12. Wintersmith, *Police and the Black Community*, 6.
13. Paul Chevigny, *Police Power* (New York: Pantheon Books, 1969), 394.
14. Goldsmith and Goldsmith, *The Police Community*, 16.
15. Chevigny, *Police Power*, 397.
16. Chevigny, *Police Power*, 397.
17. *Chicago Daily Defender*, series on police brutality, March 5–10, 1958.
18. James Ralph Jr., *Northern Protest: Martin Luther King, Chicago, and the Civil Rights Movement* (Cambridge, MA: Harvard University Press, 1993), 50.
19. William F. Roemer Jr., *Man Against the Mob* (New York: Ivy Books, 1989), 211.
20. *Chicago Sun-Times*, December 28, 1967.
21. Skolnick, *The Politics of Protest*, 260–263.
22. *Chicago Sun-Times*, December 28, 1967, front page.
23. Interview with Renault Robinson, co-founder and director of the Afro-American Patrolmen's League, August 1982. Robinson stated that this procedure was standard; this account was later confirmed by retired Chicago

police superintendent Leroy Martin in an interview conducted December 24, 1994.

24. "Klan Headquarters Claim 50 Police Officers in Chicago Police Department Belong to Klan," *Chicago Sun-Times*, December 28, 1967.

25. Ben Joravsky and Eduardo Camacho, *Race and Politics in Chicago* (Chicago: Community Renewal Society, 1988), 41.

26. Metropolitan Applied Research Center, *Search and Destroy* (New York, 1970), 16–17.

27. *Chicago Defender*, May 6, 1969.

28. *Chicago Defender*, May 8, 1969.

29. *Chicago Defender*, May 13, 1969.

30. Ralph Knoohuizen, *Police and Their Use of Fatal Force in Chicago* (Chicago: Chicago Law Enforcement Study Group, 1972), 32.

31. Knoohuizen, *Police and Their Use of Fatal Force in Chicago*, "Linda Anderson Index."

32. *Black Panther Community News Service*, July 1969.

33. *Brief for Appellants Bell, Satchell, Clark, and Truelock*, No. 77-1698, Appeals from the United States District Court for the Northern District of Illinois, Eastern Division, 12. This document is the appeal filed by attorneys representing the estate of Fred Hampton in the wrongful death lawsuit against the City of Chicago. The case was ultimately settled in favor of the plaintiffs. Hereafter cited as the *Appeals Brief*.

34. Knoohuizen, *Police and Their Use of Fatal Force in Chicago*, "Wayne Black Index."

35. Knoohuizen, *Police and Their Use of Fatal Force in Chicago*, "Maple Shorten Index."

36. Knoohuizen, *Police and Their Use of Fatal Force in Chicago*, 6–12.

37. Knoohuizen, *Police and Their Use of Fatal Force in Chicago*, conclusion.

38. Interviews with Black police officers who founded the Afro-American Patrolmen's League (AAPL), including Renault Robinson, Howard Saffold, and Edward "Buzz" Palmer, summer 1982.

39. Robinson and Saffold interview.

40. Interview with Edward "Buzz" Palmer, founding member of the Afro-American Patrolmen's League, November 1982.

41. Saffold interview.

42. Robinson and Saffold interview.

43. Robinson and Saffold interview.

44. Because the Panthers were all Black, police informants had to be Black in order to infiltrate the organization; even so, their demeanor often made them identifiable.

45. Interviews with Edward Palmer and Howard Saffold.

46. Frank Donner, *Protectors of Privilege: Red Squads and Police Repression in Urban America* (Berkeley: University of California Press, 1990), 104–105

47. *Chicago Tribune*, March 13, 1975.

48. Brooks and Jewel Cook interviews.

49. *Appeals Brief*, 12.

50. Interview with Jerry Dunigan, former head of Illinois Black Panther Party security, conducted at Danville Correctional Center, May 1994.

51. Donner, *Protectors of Privilege*, 137.

52. Interview with Paul Sequeira, photographer with the *Chicago Daily News*, conducted at his apartment on North Cleveland Avenue, Chicago, March 1982. Sequeira also donated photographs of the confrontation at the rally discussed here.

53. Interview with James Brzeczek, former Chicago police superintendent, April 1996.

54. Brooks, Cook, and Calvin interviews. Although no independent corroboration exists for this version of events, the conduct of police during the raid is consistent with observations by *Chicago Daily News* reporter Lu Palmer during a later raid in October 1969.

55. Palmer interview, 1982.

56. U.S. Senate, 94th Congress, 2nd Session, *Final Report of the Select Committee to Study Governmental Operations with Respect to Intelligence Activities*, Supplemental Detailed Staff Reports, Book III, 197. (Hereafter cited as the *Church Report*; Senator Frank Church chaired the committee.)

57. Richard Gid Powers, *Secrecy and Power: The Life of J. Edgar Hoover* (New York: Free Press, 1987), 450.

58. Powers, *Secrecy and Power*, 408; Athan G. Theoharis and John Stuart Cox, *The Boss: J. Edgar Hoover and the Great American Inquisition* (Philadelphia: Temple University Press, 1988), 277–278, 354–360. Among those Hoover regarded as potentially subversive were Albert Einstein, Owen Lattimore, Carl Sandburg, William Faulkner, and Tennessee Williams.

59. Powers, *Secrecy and Power*, 461.

60. *Church Report*, Book III, 75–78.

61. *Church Report*, Book III, 407–408.

62. *Church Report*, Book III, 461.

63. Airtel from FBI Director to Chicago Field Office regarding the West Side Organization (WSO), racial matters, dated May 17, 1968. This document refers to an earlier airtel of September 8, 1967, in which Barracuda's Black Panthers were described as a "militant Black nationalist organization." The document was obtained through the Freedom of Information Act.

64. Interview with Abraham Lincoln Rice, also known as "Barracuda," July 1984; see also personal correspondence with Gene Wilson, information

officer of the CIA, 1977–1978. *Appeals Brief,* 10. This information comes from FBI records produced during litigation after it was revealed that William O'Neal had been a paid FBI informant. The FBI had initially concealed this fact. The details appear in FBI memoranda from the Chicago field office to the director, entered into the record as Plaintiffs' Exhibits 1–121, 305, and 413.

65. *Appeals Brief,* 8–15.
66. Cook and Brooks interviews.
67. *Appeals Brief,* FBI memorandum of 1970, Plaintiffs' Exhibit 415.
68. *Appeals Brief,* FBI memoranda from Special Agent to SAC, Chicago, dated January 15 and January 28, 1969.
69. Anonymous former Panthers interviewed in 1982–1983.
70. *Appeals Brief,* 10–11.
71. Interview with Bobby Rush, former deputy minister of defense, Illinois Black Panther Party, April 1982; interview with Yvonne King, deputy minister of labor, March 1982.
72. Donner, *Protectors of Privilege,* 93–97.
73. Donner, *Protectors of Privilege,* 146–151.
74. Stanley Robinson, *The Badge They Are Trying to Bury* (Monticello, UT: Simon Belt Publishing, 1975).
75. *Chicago Tribune,* March 13, 1975; *Chicago Daily News,* February 17, 1970.

Chapter 6

The Demise of the Illinois Black Panther Party

The FBI's raid on the Illinois Black Panther Party's Headquarters in June of 1969 had taken away a significant number of Party members.[1] In addition, the harassment from the police further weakened the Party. One effective means of harassment was for the police to make false arrests, based on trumped-up charges. As a result, seventeen key Party members were charged with kidnapping and torturing someone who had stolen several weapons from the Illinois Panther Party.[2]

These seventeen were not connected with the incident, but were in strategic positions within the Party. Most of them decided to go into hiding or leave the country for a time, presumably until the charges were dropped.[3] Head of Security, Jerry Dunigan, was thereby out of Chicago and in hiding, as were several other Panther officers, including Yvonne King, Minister of Labor, and Billy Brooks, Deputy Minister of Education. For the remainder of the year, key leaders in the Illinois Panthers were in hiding or in jail. That pattern began in the Spring of 1969. The FBI raid came in June.

July heralded the split between the former members of SNCC in the Panther Party. Robert Brown, a founder of the Illinois chapter and former SNCC member, left the Illinois Panthers about this time, as did several other founding members.[4] As has been mentioned in Chapter 2, this split was over the Party's emphasis on revolution and on multiethnic alliances. The Party under Huey P. Newton's leadership remained a socialist, revolutionary party, committed to multiethnic alliances, while most of its former SNCC members preferred a Pan-African and capitalist direction.

The Mob threatened another Party leader, Drew Ferguson, who was trying to organize a boycott of stores on Madison Street, and his ardor cooled considerably.[5] While he did not leave the Party, something they said to him evidently struck home, and the Panthers could no longer count on him on a daily basis. Meanwhile, two police raids on the Black Panthers' headquarters, and the resulting shootouts, at Madison Street and Western Avenue, had made local people a little skittish about being seen with Panthers. The police raids and the Panthers' unintimidated response with gunfire had made them heroes to the local young people, but at that same time, nobody wanted to be there when the next shootout occurred.

It was heroic to shoot it out with the police, but it was not smart. To paraphrase Mao, heroism leads to conceit. Conceit leads to dogmatism. Dogmatism alienates the people.[6] The Panthers were local celebrities, but the people were content to be spectators. The Panthers, as heroes, took the admiration they received as confirmation of their correct politics. Their rationale was that since the police initiated the attack and the police are the enemies of the people, then they must have been on the correct path to revolution. They were quite capable of isolating themselves with this dogma reaching a point where many of them saw themselves as heroes, which is to say, better than the average people. This was not good politics, although the fact that they stood up to the police and shot it out with them did show the community the strength of their beliefs. However, their sincerity did not mean they were correct in the eyes of the majority of people in the community. It did, however, indicate that they had caught the attention of the local powers that be, and that these powers recognized the Panthers had potential to grow.

Adding to their isolation was the fact that some unknown people were spreading rumors about the Panthers, i.e., that they were drug-pushers, that Fred Hampton was a gambler who stole Party funds and gambled them away, that the Panthers had murdered a woman, that they were all thugs and pickpockets.[7] When the Party members went into a local bar or pool hall with the Panther newspaper, they often were asked to leave, or the owner would tell the customers not to talk with the Panther. The Panthers did not tolerate being thrown out and chose to remain and proselytize. This was their community, and they were not about to be disrespected. Nevertheless, a gap had developed between them and the community. When Hampton got out of jail on appeal in

September, he set to work healing that gap. The Illinois Panthers continued with their plans to set up a free medical clinic for Lawndale. Twenty-year-old Ronald Satchel, Deputy Minister of Health, led this project. He and his cadre raised funds and argued and cajoled doctors at County Hospital to donate time to the community. "Serve the people!" was their message, and they delivered it convincingly. By emphasizing health care for the poor, rather than their own revolutionary politics, they were able to get several doctors and nurses to come to their clinic a few hours a week and serve the people.[8] Intense, dedicated Joan Gray, twenty, and a Panther field lieutenant, ran a free legal aid clinic out of this same building on 16th Street, east of Pulaski Road.[9] Their emphasis was moving strongly toward serving the people, and downplaying guns and talk of violence, indicating they were aware that it was necessary to adjust to local conditions. However, police provocation was still a strong reality. They had dared to challenge police authority, and there were Chicago police officers who were not about to let them forget it.

The corner of Washington and Hoyne Streets was a dangerous corner, only a few blocks from Panther headquarters, where two children had been hit by cars that September. Consistent community protests for weeks had accomplished nothing.

Hampton brought the Panthers into the fray:

> It was Huey P. Newton who taught us how the people learn. You learn by participation. When Huey P. Newton started out, what did he do? He got a gun, and he got Bobby, and Bobby got a gun. They had a problem in the community because people were being run over–kids were being run over–at a certain intersection. What did the people do? The people went down to the government to redress their grievances, and the government told them to go to hell...What did Huey P. Newton do? Did he go out and tell the people about the laws, and to write letters? No! Some of that is good, but the masses of the people don't write–that's what I heard him say–they learn through observation and participation. Did he just say this? No! So what did he do? He got him a shotgun, he got Bobby, and he got him a hammer and went down to the corner...and nailed up a stop sign. No more accidents...What did the people do? They looked at it, they observed, they didn't get a chance to participate in it. Next time, what did they do?... The PEOPLE got their shotguns, got their nine

millimeters, got their hammers. How they learn? They learned
by observation and participation.[10]

The situation at Hoyne and Washington Streets was obviously parallel
to this one. It was a means for the Illinois Panther Party to reaffirm its
stand with the community. When the community petition for a stoplight
was ignored, the Panther Party took the lead. The Panthers stood in the
street and stopped traffic, unarmed. Fred Hampton's actions were more
often pragmatic and less dramatic than his rhetoric.

The people of Henry Horner Projects imitated the Panthers, and their
massive civil disobedience won them a stoplight. Given the climate
between the community and the police, particularly where the Panthers
were involved, the police were not happy with this show of clout. What
followed provides evidence that a group of police were perhaps taking
things into their own hands.

Two of the most identifiable people involved in the stoplight protest
were the half-Puerto Rican, half-black Soto boys, Michael, twenty-one,
and John, sixteen. They stood out because they looked Latino rather than
"black." Sunday night, the 5th of October, around 10:00 p.m., John Soto
was shot and killed by police officer John Nolan. Officer Nolan claimed
the youth lunged at him and he shot in self-defense. Eyewitnesses said he
shot the boy in cold blood, without provocation. Evidence suggests the
local resident's version is correct, as the boy was shot in the back of the
head.[11] The neighborhood was angry and tense, and next day's news did
not help. The police had accidentally killed a two-year-old girl, Rosina
Marbley, in the Cabrini-Green Housing Project, while shooting at snipers,
three miles to the northeast of Henry Homer Homes.[12]

John Soto's older brother, Michael, was an Army sergeant, home on
leave from the war in Vietnam. He had been deeply involved in the
stoplight protests. The killing of his brother gave birth to a committee
protesting police killings of black people–in which he involved himself.
Michael asked for an extension on his leave to arrange for his brother's
funeral. Friday, October 10, 1969, there was a supposed robbery near the
Henry Horner Homes, and the suspects were chased into the projects,
according to police.

Officer Robert Rahn chased Michael Soto to a landing of his building
and shot him dead, the police said. Eyewitnesses said Soto was standing
on the landing talking to police when the officer shot him in cold blood.
Officer Rahn had killed another young man a week previously.

Eyewitnesses said Michael was unarmed.[13] As Sgt. Michael Soto, war hero, lay dying, police converged on the scene, while at the same time, the word of his "murder" spread throughout Henry Horner Homes (two blocks from Panther headquarters). While the residents may have had little enthusiasm for revolution, this provocation was one too many for the local residents. The Panther Party had already shown them the police were not supermen, and now they, like their cousins down South with the Klan, began to shoot at the police. The police responded with indiscriminate machine gun fire into the housing project. When the battle ended, two hours later, nine police were wounded, and the police had, with massive indiscriminate firing into the buildings, killed an 11-year-old girl.[14] This was the Chicago Police Department, at its very worst, alienating the community. In the weeks that followed the Soto brothers' killings, police harassed several eyewitnesses to the crime out of the neighborhood. The Panthers called for a decentralized, community-controlled police force.

The investigations into these particular killings of the Soto brothers were hampered, according to the State Attorney's Office, led by State's Attorney Edward Hanrahan, by the distrust of black people for the District Attorney. Somehow, the D.A.'s office said, the neighborhood residents felt the State's Attorney and the Chicago Police Department were one and the same.[15] The facts, however, substantiate that belief.

Of some seventy-nine cases of police killings of civilians in the years 1969 and 1970, neither eyewitness accounts of police murdering citizens, nor evidence that contradicted the police, nor contradictions between police, brought one police officer to court. Yet the States Attorney had reviewed every case.[16] Early the next year (1970), States Attorney Hanrahan dropped the Soto brothers' case, blaming the black community's lack of trust in his office. At the same time, he was in fact acting with the police to cover up a murderous shootout of a sleeping member of the Black Panther Party, by Chicago police assigned to his office.[17] So, the community had been essentially correct; the State's Attorney's Office and the police acted as one.

The Soto brothers' killing underlined the tension already present between the poor black community of the West Side and the Chicago Police Department and strengthened the Panthers' appeal throughout Chicago's poor communities. The Soto deaths probably had a stronger emotional effect on members of the Panther Party, having involved themselves in so many cases of alleged police brutality. Several members of the Black Panther Party were soon patrolling the alleys of their neighborhood with weapons in their hands, inviting the police to come arrest them.[18] At the same time, the Party, nationally, was attempting to tone down its rhetoric.[19] That summer had been a deadly one for Black Panthers across the country. Nevertheless, the atmosphere, particularly in Chicago, was charged with anger. The Panthers, probably to a person, felt they were targets for trigger-happy police and were in a highly provoked state of mind.

Nineteen-year-old Jake Winters, in November 1969, was not peculiar in the rage he felt against the Chicago Police. However, the Panther Party had kept his rage under control. Winters believed totally in the Panther Party and immersed himself in it. Jake Winters was peculiar in that he was also a lover of guns. Evidently, that got him in trouble with his cadre leader.[20]

Around the end of the first week in November, Winters had a serious disagreement with his cadre leader, Bobby Rush. Rush wanted Jake expelled from the Party following this altercation, and Rush got his way. It was a bitter pill for young Winters to accept. One week later, when he might have been getting his head together for the college scholarship he had received to Xavier University, he was, instead, walking around the South Side neighborhood of his boyhood, angry and distraught.[21] He and Lance "Santa Claus" Bell, a Party member, had a hideout there in the abandoned Washington Park Hotel, located at 58th Street and Calumet Avenue. A jail guard from Cook County Jail had taken a gun from them earlier that day, and they wanted it back.

They hung around his house across from the hotel until the Jail guard's wife, home alone, got nervous and called the police. Lance Bell evidently left. When the police arrived, they came down 58th Street from the east and surrounded the hotel from the side Winters could not see. Had they come from the west or down Calumet, he would have seen them early, and he would probably have fled.[22] Now they surrounded the building, and Winters was inside, trapped. Jake Winters was well aware of what had happened to Panther Larry Roberson and to the Soto brothers. He kept two rifles in the hotel and plenty of ammunition. The situation was loaded, weighted down by the history of police in the Chicago black ghetto, and perhaps, it was inevitable.

Jake Winters had witnessed, almost intimately, the deaths of perhaps a dozen citizens at the hands of Chicago police that summer and fall, and that also must have influenced his initial act of violence. The fact that the city, the courts and the D.A. had done nothing to rectify these killings undoubtedly influenced him. As the first police officer approached the abandoned hotel, Winters fired his carbine and killed that officer. Then, as more police arrived, Jake Winters ran from empty room to empty room, firing bursts of automatic fire and single shots. Wynters virtually demolished five police cars and wounded nine police. They fired back at what seemed to be three or four people.

One war veteran police officer said it was hotter than any fight he had seen in Vietnam.[23] Jake Winters was wounded and bleeding badly about twenty minutes after the fight began, when he escaped from the gangway exit on the east end of the old building, into the cold, snow-flurried night, heading to the alley in back, then down the alley. His wound left a trail that the police picked up. It led into a dark backyard with a tunnel, which is known in Chicago as a gangway, under the only building on that block that had a gangway leading through to King Drive. Once on the other side, Winters probably could have escaped into the wide, wooded expanses of Washington Park.[24] This was his neighborhood. He obviously knew the layout. Instead, he climbed the stairs of the building and waited, gun in hand, for the first officer who came through the tunnel.

Winters was not going to plead for mercy, nor try to escape, for when that unlucky officer came through, Winters shot him, then dropped into the path of coming police officers to shoot him again as he pleaded for his life. Winters fired again, into the officer's face, before he was gunned down.[25]

It was November 13, 1969, and police provocation had cost two officers their lives, and at the time, who knew what else it would cost? The most stunning aspect of this shootout was the way Winters behaved, content to die killing police. Winters had acted more like one of those unrepentant rebels at the end of the Civil War than like an urban, college-bound Negro. What had changed him? The Panther Party had given him pride, and a summer and fall of police provocation and the lack of response from the system had given him rage when he saw people abused. Whether the police were willing to admit it or not (I have been unable to find an official word on it), the Panthers herein presented the police with a unique problem. "Decent" kids did not, until November 1969, shoot at police. The police needed to get control over those officers in their ranks who were using deadly violence as a means of control or crush this radical organization out of existence, or both. Those persons who had been violent with police prior to the Panther Party had shot in fear, with guilt,

and were disowned by their own community. This was not the case with
the Panthers. They had rage and a fervor in their cause. Community
people cared about them and got angry when they were hunted like
criminals. The local community recognized that they were not criminals.
They may have found them to be dogmatic, arrogant, even bullies at
times, but not criminal. The black community, as a mass, began to
question the legitimacy of the police. Self-respect had produced rage at
the situation they were in, which otherwise might not have occurred.
Now there was potential for more actions like this one. If the situation
were allowed to continue, attitudes like Jake Winters' might spread
throughout the black community. However, as of November 1969, only
the local West Side community had an accurate understanding of who the
Panthers were. The Chicago news media had effectively blocked that
description from reaching a broader public.

Role of the Media in Isolating the Panther Party

A look at the major, daily newspapers between 1969 and 1972 reveals
a media that was often biased; sometimes intentionally, sometimes not. A
significant revelation is their lack of concern about accuracy and an
interest in sensationalizing. Some of this blatantly poor reporting was
clearly a product of a class and/or race bias. An example of this bias is the
Chicago Sun-Times' treatment of the FBI's raid on Panther Party
headquarters on June 4, 1969. Art Petacque's story was nothing less than
the FBI's story. The FBI raided the Panther office, they said, looking for a
fugitive, George Sams. Sams, it later turned out, was an informant of
theirs in an East Coast Panther Chapter, but was not there–as O'Neal may
have related to the FBI. What the FBI found were photos of Sams, and,
the story goes on, they "recovered a cache" of weapons. Several ways in
which the article was written raise questions about its objectivity. A
trained reporter would ask why the Panthers were taking photos of Sams.

Secondly, two words were obviously leading the public to think a
certain way about the Panthers–"recovered" and "cache." "Recovered"
implies the guns were stolen, which they weren't. The word "cache"
implies the guns were hidden. Again, they were not. Thirdly, the FBI took
the guns, along with several thousand dollars and a list of volunteers.[26]
The unbiased story should have said the FBI had committed a theft, as
they never returned the money and guns. This fact did not make the news
story. Giving him the benefit of the doubt, perhaps Art Petacque did not

think a story about some poor, leftist group was worth much effort. His may have reflected a middle-class bias.

Whereas biases make for stories that are not purposely misleading, propaganda was a part of the local news media's coverage of the Panthers. Take, as an example, this lead from the *Chicago Sun-Times* on April 3, 1969:

> A Black Panther plot to bomb five Manhattan department stores on Thursday during the Easter shopping rush has been broken up by indictment of 21 members of the militant Negro group, District Attorney Frank S. Hogan said Wednesday.

The early prominence of the words "Black Panther" and the tardiness with which this paragraph is identified as a quotation from a prosecuting attorney is classic propaganda. Generally, news stories are written to contain all pertinent information in the first few lines, based on the assumption that is all the reader sees. The average reader would not even get the fact that this story is not fact, but hearsay from prosecutors, in a "plot" that did not exist anywhere but in the District Attorney's imagination. The story leads readers to think that the Panthers were terrorists.

Then there was further selective reporting in the Chicago newspapers. The Panthers' Free Breakfast for Children program began in April of 1969 and spread across the city, into Rockford and Peoria. However, despite all the coverage the Panthers got about shootouts with police, I could only find a single story about the social programs of the Party in the Chicago newspapers of 1969. That story ran above a story on gangs.

Panthers' free breakfasts for children did not make the news, yet on June 11, 1969, with a prominent sub-headline, the *Sun-Times* carried a story that the Illinois legislature had approved (not begun) free lunches for children. It might well be that the legislature's actions were in response to the Panthers' free breakfast programs.

The newspapers wanted the public to believe the Panthers were violent people. They quote a Cook County State's Attorney who reported to the news media that the Party purchased eight thousand dollars worth of guns in two years.[27] Given the size of the organization, one hundred to two hundred people–minus the two thousand dollars worth of guns the FBI stole from them, that does not translate into a large number of weapons, perhaps no more than eighty guns. Compared to the arms holdings of the Blackstone Rangers, the Ku Klux Klan, the American Nazi

Party, the local Legion of Justice, or, with one Chicago police officer in the Ku Klux Klan named Donald Heath,[28] the holdings of the Panther Party can be seen more as symbolic. Reporters neglected to ask them how much money was spent by the Illinois Panther Party on social programs. Nor did the reporters inquire into the reasons why Panthers purchase guns or their stance on the rights of citizens to own guns. Reporters opted to sensationalize rather than delve deeper into the larger issues and motivations of the Black Panthers.

The *Chicago Sun-Times* also used pejorative labels, innuendoes and the circular reasoning that if one is harassed by the police, that person is probably doing something illegal: "Fred Hampton was familiar to the police. He had been charged more than a half-dozen times with mob action, aggravated battery and disorderly conduct as he angrily pressed the militant program of the Black Panther Party."[29]

This paragraph involved nothing but misleading statements. First is the circular rationale: being charged over a half-dozen times (how many times is that, seven?) implies guilt, yet every one of these charges had been dropped for lack of evidence. They were, in fact, trumped-up charges.

Further, the mob action charge had been a standard weapon of the Democratic Party against rioters in the previous year because it provided for up to a year in prison, though it was a misdemeanor. It was also accompanied by bail ten times higher than normal, which violated an Illinois law requiring that misdemeanor bonds be no more than double the maximum fine.[30] Maybe that kind of harassment and the police killings of civilians were what made Hampton appear angry. When this story was printed, Hampton had just been killed by Chicago police officers. Apparently, the *Sun-Times* was attempting to justify the killing.

Generally speaking, the image of the Panthers was an irrational, angry, violent one in the Chicago press. Either inexperienced or biased reporters derived a large part of their image from the stories by police. The press ignored analyses and avoided stories that might have explained the escalating violence between black people and members of the Chicago Police Department.

The resignation of Lu Palmer, a black journalist of the *Chicago Daily News*, was significant. When Palmer asked to report on the community services of the Illinois Black Panther Party, he was told the *Daily News* had to protect its public from certain realities. Palmer quit the *Daily News* and founded his own newspaper.[31]

The Assassination

Former Police Superintendents Leroy Martin and James Brzeczek both described the raid on Hampton's apartment, which resulted in his death, as a "botched job," to quote former Police Superintendent Martin.[32] Brzeczek also stated that the State's Attorney was "duped" by the FBI into committing a raid that put him in serious trouble with the black community. The last half of this statement is true—the raid did damage the State's Attorney's already tarnished reputation in the black community. However, the facts also clearly indicate this was a purposeful, carefully planned and well-executed raid, which did exactly what some city officials and FBI officials in Chicago planned for it to do: kill Panther leader Hampton. The facts speak rather clearly that this was an assassination, carried out by picked assassins who happened to be police, under the direct control of a politically elected leader. Furthermore, in the history of Chicago's poor, this assassination by the powers that be was not unusual, but followed a pattern in the way it was carried out.

From the Haymarket hangings of 1884, through the killings of Octavius Granady in 1929, and Ben Lewis in 1963, (to name just a few victims of the Chicago establishment's intolerance for political dissent), murders with the aid of or by handpicked police (from Captain Bonfield of the 1880s through Officer Edward Carmody of 1969) has been one of the tools by which democracy has been subverted in Chicago. When Chicago politicians wanted someone killed, they looked to their police. What makes this case peculiar is that Hampton had reached out to other communities, and his death grabbed the attention of a cadre of excellent lawyers, willing to work without pay, who attempted to get some recourse to justice. In their attempt at justice, they exposed the full story—so it was not just another "poor-assed nigger" dead on Friday night. I will only highlight that story here. Most of this data comes from the FBI's own files, which were uncovered by the Panthers' lawyers and exposed in court.

Following the shootout that left ex-Panther Jake Winters and two police officers dead, the FBI's Roy Mitchell brought gruesome photos of the two slain police officers to his Panther informant, William O'Neal and pressured O'Neal for a detailed layout of Fred Hampton's apartment. Until this time, O'Neal had evidently tried to play both ends, being a loyal Panther, while impressing his Panther friends with the money he received from the FBI. That is to say, O'Neal's misinformation to the FBI was apparently something he did to protect the people he thought of as friends in the Black Panther Party. He evidently felt he could be a Panther and an informant and go along so that no one would get hurt, but he would get rich. However, O'Neal was an informant, and now he had to commit that one act, that drawing, that might get some of his "friends" killed. He had to do it, or the FBI would expose him to his friends. He made a detailed drawing showing where doors and windows were, where the furniture was placed and pointing out exactly where Fred Hampton slept.[33] He also gave Mitchell a list of the weapons kept at the apartment, all legal, and asked Mitchell to promise not to do anything without telling him first. O'Neal was not mentally slow. He must have known how empty this agreement was and how powerless he was. He had betrayed his "friends," and Hampton was, more likely than not, being set up for death. O'Neal had crossed the line from which there was no return, and his actions from this point on were more deadly.

FBI agent Roy Mitchell went to the Cook County State's Attorney's office, under the elected State's Attorney Edward Hanrahan, and spoke with Hanrahan's appointee, Richard Jalovec. Hanrahan and Jalovec had recruited a selection of police officers, screened and interviewed by them, who were unique in that they answered only to a civilian; that was Jalovec. Both Hanrahan and Jalovec knew that several of the police officers they had recruited had several disciplinary complaints against them, including the notoriously brutal James "Gloves" Davis, so nicknamed by the black community for his habit of putting on gloves before administering a beating. Both William O'Neal and Bobby Rush said in court that Davis had a reputation for terrorizing black people.[34]

According to former Superintendent Brzeczek, the Gang Intelligence Unit of the Chicago Police Department had previously been urged to raid the Panther apartment where Hampton slept, but were too smart to be "suckered" in by the FBI.[35] Mitchell told Jalovec that there were riot shotguns at the apartment. He also told Jalovec that Hampton's appeal on the ice cream truck robbery had been denied and that he would be ordered to return to jail soon. On the 1st of December, Mitchell purportedly lied by telling Jalovec that an illegal sawed-off shotgun and a stolen police shotgun were at the apartment, gave him O'Neal's floor plan and suggested a raid. Here was a false pretense to stage a raid (stolen guns) and a means to facilitate its effectiveness. Mitchell later denied this accusation and said, as his informant O'Neal had related to him, all the weapons in the apartment on Monroe were legally owned.[36] So the ostensible purpose of the raid was to seize contraband that law

124

enforcement's only informant said did not exist. The warrant for the raid was itself invalid. To be valid, under Illinois law, it would have required the signature of the provider of the information, namely, Roy Mitchell. His signature was not there.[37]

The FBI had already raided Panther headquarters once, as previously described. They had come in at dawn with a bullhorn and tear gas, and they had phoned ahead. The Panthers had surrendered without a shot. Clearly, this raid, whose purpose was, supposedly, to seize stolen weapons (which did not exist), could have been a carbon copy of that one, if that was what they actually wanted to accomplish. Regular surveillance of the Panthers also made them knowledgeable of the Panthers' schedule, which included political education classes every Wednesday at 8:00 p.m. until 10:30 p.m., presumably a good time for a weapons raid. These police, however, were being led to do what they may already have wanted to do.

During the evening of December 3, 1969, the leader, Sgt. Daniel Groth got permission from Jalovec to take a machine gun on this raid, although he had never taken one on any previous raid of gang weapons ''warehouses." He also got permission to use fourteen men, although no previous raid had ever been more than eight men. These fourteen were allowed to take along personal weapons. They included two men who were friends of the officers killed by Jake Winters, three weeks previously. State's Attorney Hanrahan admitted in court to knowing this fact. "Gloves" Davis also took along hollow-point dum-dum bullets. No teargas, no bullhorn, no floodlights, no phone calls were considered. In fact, the raiders got the telephone company to supply them with a truck and to turn off the phone at the apartment. The Chicago Police Department was notified of the raid about five minutes before it happened.[38]

The raid occurred at 4:30 a.m. when the occupants were asleep. Perhaps the police knocked. Two of the occupants remembered a knock, while several others did not. However, the raiders did come in shooting. The police raiders shot ninety-nine bullets into the apartment.[39] One shot may have come from a Panther gun, and that one shot most probably occurred as their guard behind the front door, Mark Clark, was being shot in the heart by "Gloves" Davis, with a shotgun in his hand. No other Panther (there were nine in the apartment) fired a shot. It is clear from the court record that the apartment was secured and in complete control of the police when the two deadliest shots were fired.

Two bullets to a sleeping Fred Hampton's face, at point-blank range, killed him.[40] He had apparently never awakened. And evidence strongly suggests that O'Neal had drugged him with Seconal.[41] Panther field Lieutenant Ronald "Doc" Satchel was wounded five times and was later to need his colon removed. Verlina Brewer was shot in the back of the knee, the bullet exploding out the front. Blair Anderson was shot in the penis. One officer was injured, Edward Carmody. Carmody, the officer who executed the assassination, cut his hand breaking in the back door. The surviving occupants were rounded up, cursed, shoved outside and taken away, and promptly charged with attempted murder of police officers attempting to serve a warrant.[42]

Perhaps the most startling fact about this entire execution was the boldness and the arrogance with which the raiding police officers murdered two men. They did not once consider looking at Hampton after the shooting had stopped. He was dead, and that was that. Nor did they consider sealing off the place where they had done their deed, nor taking any care with the weapons they seized. Sgt. Groth, in fact, told the crime lab not to dust the seized weapons for fingerprints. Nor did the officers record whether any of these weapons had been fired, or if there were unexpended rounds inside the chambers.[43] Clearly, they walked out of that apartment and expected to walk away with no questions asked. If this type of operation were not standard procedure, or if they had not been given every assurance that they would not be prosecuted, one could presume they would have covered themselves far better than they did.

It is interesting to speculate whether the entire team was told this was an execution. Possibly, they were not told. Possibly, if fourteen police officers with violent reputations are assembled, armed, allowed to carry extra weapons, given no tear gas, and ordered to serve a warrant at 4:30 a.m.–with a floor plan that denotes where one person on that floor plan sleeps–they can figure out what is wanted from them. An airtel from the Chicago FBI office to Hoover's D.C. office, sent to request a bonus for William O'Neal for his part in the "success" of this raid, certainly makes plain that the FBI wanted Hampton dead.[44]

State's Attorney Hanrahan, under criticism almost immediately for the violent methods used in the Hampton raid, had his police act out their version of the raid. In their version, the police came under heavy fire and begged for the Panthers to surrender, to which the only reply from the Panthers was "shoot it out." However, from the place where these Panthers supposedly shot, there were no spent shells, and the direction in which they supposedly aimed had no bullet holes in the walls, and no police were hit in the cramped little apartment where the "shootout" occurred. Nevertheless, CBS television ran the police story on the evening news. After four years of trial, the "shootout" was finally exposed for the assassination it was. Of some ninety-nine shots fired in this raid, ninety-eight were traceable to a police officer's gun (the ninety-ninth shot could not be traced to a particular gun). It was also in 1973 when FBI agent provocateur William O'Neal was exposed as the person who made Hampton's execution possible. O'Neal was testifying for the government against police Sgt. Stanley Robinson, that he was present when Robinson killed two black businessmen. Sgt. Robinson said O'Neal had done the killings. Either way, the fact that O'Neal was testifying on behalf of the government in that trial meant he was probably working for the government in other areas. This was the key that unlocked his role as agent provocateur inside the Illinois Panther Party.[45]

That was in the future. As of January 1970, seven Panthers were in jail for attempted murder. Their charismatic leader was dead, the last of the leaders they generally admired, and paranoia was escalating among the Panthers. A raid on Lynn French's apartment, on December 2, 1969, in which she, seven months pregnant, had failed to meet the police with gunfire (Huey Newton's executive order no. 3), was met with criticism among leaderless Panthers. Lynn French was punched several times by police officers, kicked in her stomach and taken to jail. Nevertheless, she got no accolades for her determination.[46] The Panthers of 1970 were dedicated, angry, isolated and suspicious of anyone and everyone. Fred Hampton was dead, and everyone was certain a spy had made his killing possible.[47] Necessarily, they asked, which one of us is the spy?[48] They got a mass of sympathy from the black community, but very few new members. They continued with their fervent message, "All Power to the People!" but the less radical activists in that society did not want the risk of Panther association, even as the Panthers moved to moderate their politics. The death of its charismatic leader and the fact that he had been betrayed spelled the end of the fervent, revolutionary Illinois Black Panther Party.

OVERKILL BY THE FBI

The Illinois Black Panther Party, as a radical revolutionary group, was extinct. Both the moderate leadership of Bobby Rush and the moderation of the Panther Party in Oakland were riding out the storm of deaths, intimidation and ideological splintering fostered by the FBI. The Illinois

Party was getting a sudden abundance of sympathy from the middle class for what it had so far endured; it was being nurtured, but the spirit was dying. The intensity of the government's reaction was too much for it to exist as it had. While Deputy Minister Rush tried to moderate, he was losing the warriors. The people who had come into the Party had not done so to become reformers. Within the next year, most of these warriors were gone. This was a new Panther Party emerging from the deaths of 1969, but the federal government, alarmed at the way the wider black community suddenly supported the Panthers, continued and even intensified its attack.

O'Neal had not yet done his dirtiest in Chicago. Those deeds would come in 1970. He would be involved in the killings of five more people; one of these murders, the lethal overdose of the wife of an Illinois Panther, was probably his own work. He would also sell illegal drugs in the black suburb of Maywood with the FBI's knowledge.[49]

Throughout the year 1970, the Panther Party formed sympathetic groups in the high schools of the black community (and to an extent in the Latino community). On the one-year anniversary of the murder of Fred Hampton, they demonstrated their muscle.

Chairman Bobby Rush called for a high-school boycott, of school and it went off as planned. At Crane High School, near Panther headquarters, the entire student body came to school just so they could walk out, and, on cue, 1,300 students marched out of the doors. Neither teachers nor police could stop them. The same thing happened at Harlan, Hyde Park, Englewood, Calumet, Hirsch, and South Shore High Schools. All of those students who bothered to come walked out of Kenwood, Dunbar, Phillips, Marshall, Bowen, Harrison, Fenger, and Austin High Schools. Students and the police clashed at Calumet, and at Chicago Vocational High School—a riot erupted between police and students.[50] These students did not just take a holiday. Five thousand of them attended two rallies honoring Hampton, and several hundred marched on Chicago Police Headquarters. However, this proved to be the Illinois Panther Party's last show of political muscle as a revolutionary political party. The Panther Party moved from its home base, the West Side, to the far more conservative South Side, where a working black political machine and a depressed and alienated populace left it vulnerable and isolated. Its bus, for taking relatives to visit the prisons, was rammed several times, and eventually, they were unable to repair it. Its Free Breakfast Program was poorly attended.[51] Moreover, its more talented members were ordered to

Oakland to shore up the original Panther Party's bid for an elected city council seat. Finally, its printing press was delivered to the Oakland chapter. The Illinois Panther Party ceased to exist in the spring of 1974, although, in fact, it had been near death since 1971.[52]

The FBI program of disruption continued into the 1970s. William O'Neal, about to be expelled from the Panther Party, had introduced a drug operation in Maywood, Illinois, perhaps its very first. In 1970, Jerry Dunigan, one of the staunchest remaining Party members, lost his wife. She had become hooked on heroin. How she had gotten hooked was a mystery to Jerry Dunigan, called "Odinga" by Party members. He simply remembers that when he came back from hiding over a trumped-up criminal charge against him, she was an addict.[53] He put her in Henrotin Hospital. Then he went to the supposedly "hip" O'Neal and asked him about it. It was O'Neal who had supplied her, but Odinga did not have the faintest notion of that, and it is logical to assume O'Neal had to keep it that way. He first pointed out to Dunigan the apartment complex where, he said, her drug dealers lived. Then, in a style that had become typical of him, he urged Dunigan to not "be a punk" and wreak vengeance on them.[54] Shortly thereafter, someone fitting O'Neal's description slipped into Dianne Dunigan's room in Henrotin. Dianne Dunigan died of a drug overdose, and it was a drug the hospital was not giving her.[55]

Jerry Dunigan, in 1970, was an intelligent, articulate man with a great deal of anger in him, just below his surface cool. William O'Neal probably perceived that. Dunigan came under intense harassment, according to his friends. They say you could not walk down the street with him without witnessing him being harassed by police officers.[56] It is possible that O'Neal felt he could push Dunigan over the edge, and that is apparently what happened to him. The death of his wife on December 24, 1970, his having four young children without a mother, and the constant harassment by the police certainly contributed to his temporary insanity. Off and on, over that past year, since the murder of Hampton, Dunigan had, so his friends report, acted queerly. On the night after his wife's death, December 25, 1970, he lost it all, accosting an innocent man and his wife in the building O'Neal had pointed out to him as the drug dealers'. Jerry Dunigan tied the man up and attacked his wife, taunting the man as he did it. "How does it feel to have to watch this?" Then Dunigan shot her in the head and fled into the night.[57]

All three innocent victims, Diane Dunigan, and Agnes and Leo

Silverstein, were the victims of William O'Neal's warped brain and COINTELPRO (which had placed O'Neal in the Party to wreak havoc), and the Chicago Office of the FBI. Odinga, captured after seven years in hiding, is now serving a three-hundred-year sentence. Neither O'Neal, for causing Diane Dunigan's death, nor any FBI officials have ever been indicted. Bringing Cold War tactics home to use on American citizens had deadly repercussions, but it has been sanctioned, if tacitly, by the failure of the government to punish anyone for the crimes those government officials committed.

Also, in the summer of 1970, a 19-year-old Panther Omowale X. Babatunde supposedly blew himself up on the Illinois Central Railroad tracks. He was supposedly trying to blow up the tracks, according to police,[58] but other facts make that accusation questionable. Babatunde reported that someone had tried to kill him the previous month by removing all the lug nuts on his tires. Babatunde was a Panther not known for any violent propensities.[59] Finally, the tracks themselves were untouched. Clearly, intensified harassment and paranoia were producing desperate behavior. Perhaps Babatunde did try to blow up the tracks. However, the Panthers believed that he was assassinated.[60] Another Illinois Panther, Jimmy Brewster, hijacked a plane and fled to Cuba about this time.[61]

The atmosphere that caused such mental anguish was produced, at least in part, by the government. The federal intelligence agencies anticipated a revolution and went about destroying it without waiting to see if it was possible, without waiting to see how the black American community would react to the message of revolution. They admittedly dishonored their own rules, the laws of the land.

Meanwhile, the Chicago Police Department took advantage of their legal abuses to weaken their own critics with massive spying and criminal behavior, encouraging burglaries and promoting assaults by right-wing radicals on SDS and other anti-police or anti-war groups.[62] The police, therefore, did not respect the law. Street hustlers, witnessing the police's disregard for the law, took advantage of the situation and abused their fellow citizens. Any opportunist could "spy" on any organization, find them to be subversive and collect money. Organizationally, the neighborhood of South Austin suffered as its strongest community group, the Organization for a Better Austin, was destroyed by the distrust and ill will spread by a police spy. The sanctioning of rough tactics could, and did, spread into any modest community group that opposed, for example, a liquor store allowed to open near a school and across from a park, in violation of a city ordinance, on Van Buren and Central Streets in 1974. The community protest leader's house was suddenly on fire.[63] The liquor store opened. In short, innocent citizens paid the accumulated bill, victims of a criminal mentality funded by the FBI and promoted by the Chicago Police Department's Red Squad.

The FBI had missed its aim badly. As popular as Hampton was locally, and as charismatic and courageous as the Panthers were, very few black citizens over the age of thirty considered revolution a viable option for America in 1969. If Hampton had been left alone, it seems there would not have been an outpouring of sympathy for the Illinois Panthers. They were, at that time, losing their supporters. Moreover, the Panther Party had been good at serving the needs of the local community. Nevertheless, it was not the cry of revolution that people responded to, but their affirmative attitude, their sincerity.

The idea that Marxist intellectuals used, about heightening the contradictions of capitalism, meant very little to the reality of black Chicagoans. So many black Chicagoans lived off the contradictions, the inconsistencies of the system. "Now what is this socialism you all talking about?" a middle-aged woman at the Center for Inner-City Studies wanted to know. After the Panther explained, she said, "Oh, y'all mean sharing! Well, why don't you just call it that?"[64] The Panther did not answer. The point is that black Chicagoans responded to the Panther Party in 1969 the same way they responded to the Communist Party in 1939. That response was also the same way they responded to the Garvey movement of 1929. That response was geared to whether they were doing some good for that community. If they were, then they were not shunned. There were black people in the Garvey movement who switched to the Communist Party quite easily, although the messages these two groups espoused were diametrically opposite. There were people in the Communist Party who worked with conservative black Congressman William Dawson. It did not take a genius to see that the support for the Black Panther Party was of this same nature.

If the FBI had had a competent spy (not a provocateur) in the Panther Party, if they even hired black agents, they could have seen how effective they had already been. However, they did not. They went after 21-year-old Fred Hampton like he was a threat to the United States. I would dare to speculate that the only way he could become a threat would be as a martyr. What did the government fear? I sense the government feared change, creative, unpredictable thoughts, the kind that are a necessary part of adaptation. However, when you inhibit change, you ensure malfunction. The West Side community was in far worse shape in the late 1970s than it had been in the late 1960s. The black community, particularly the West Side community, got a course in governmental oppression from the city and the national government in the years 1968 through 1973. One should expect that they, and all witnesses to that oppression, would have a fundamentally different view of Chicago (and Chicago police) and the nation, than those who'd remained unaware of that experience or untouched by it.

Furthermore, there are many great things about Chicago: its beautiful lakefront; its engineering skills that turned the Chicago River backward; or built the Deep Tunnel for draining the swamp it would sit in; its material plenty for all; and its rewards for those who excel. However, their response to those who dared to dissent, particularly if they were black and poor, has historically been violent and undemocratic. The history of the Illinois Panther Party was a powerful example of that undemocratic, violent and intolerant spirit.

The Illinois Black Panther Party had not been a failure. In boldly asserting the right to consider revolution as an option, it had produced powerful changes in the Chicago black electorate. For the first time in history, a large portion of the black community split its vote, crossed over to vote for the Republican candidate for State's Attorney Bernard Carey. Republican Carey won thirteen of fourteen black wards. State's Attorney Edward Hanrahan's career, which had been on the rise, was shot dead by his ordering of the raid on Black Panther leader Fred Hampton's apartment that resulted in Hampton's death. For the first time in Chicago's history, Chicago's Black Member of Congress, it was then Ralph Metcalfe, was able to defy the Democratic Party over the issue of police brutality and survive politically, as an aroused electorate defied the black committeemen who battled for Daley against Metcalfe.[65] None of the perpetrators of Hampton's murder were ever indicted, but our democracy did provide some repercussions for the oppression and murder of citizens by authorities.

The city was forced to pay the families of Fred Hampton and Mark Clark almost two million dollars for their wrongful deaths.[66] More intangibly, but just as real, the Panthers left a legacy of pride. Young blacks, growing up in Chicago, were raised to be proud that there were young black men and women willing to risk their lives battling brutal

132

police, to give up years of their personal lives to feed hungry children, to go into neighborhoods that were hostile to blacks, or hostile to them for their politics, and to shout defiance at the disrespect the city politics gave poor people.

That there was a Panther Party made it possible to have a comfort about being black. It mattered little whether their politics were astute or not.

Summation

The fervor of the Panther movement in Chicago was created in the oppressive political atmosphere of Chicago's black West Side. There, poor, uprooted people had not been able to find a vehicle for expressing their fight against those who kept them politically powerless. These forces included the Cook County Democratic Party's "West Side bloc" and their politically favored police who intimidated independent political movements.

The Illinois Panther Party had successfully attracted the young, politically ambitious youth of that community. However, the Panther Party's focus in their rhetoric was on national revolution, even if they directed their actions locally with the community and against the police. Since their rhetoric was anti-federal government, it was the alignment of the federal agency, the FBI, that is, and the police, in their determination to get rid of the Panther Party, that brought about the Illinois Black Panther Party's destruction as an effective political party. Their own youthful mistakes pushed this demise along.

Notes

1. Bobby Rush, co-founder of the Illinois Black Panther Party, estimated that the FBI raid reduced active Party membership by nearly half. Former Panther Joan Gray agreed in an interview conducted November 1996 that the raid caused a significant decline in membership.
2. Interview with former Illinois Panther Jerry Dunigan, April 16, 1992.
3. Jerry Dunigan and Yvonne King fled to Canada by separate routes. Several others went into hiding in Chicago. They became known as the "Panther Seventeen." Charges against most of these Party members were eventually dropped.
4. The Student Nonviolent Coordinating Committee (SNCC) disbanded around this time.
5. Interview with Joseph Shaw, January 1996. The Panther in question was Drew Ferguson.
6. Mao Tse-tung, *Quotations from Chairman Mao Tse-tung* (Peking: Foreign Languages Press, 1972), 181.
7. While volunteering in the Free Breakfast for Children Program, the author was approached by individuals who recounted stories similar to those described here, often when he was alone or leaving a program site.
8. Interviews with Joan Gray (November 1996) and Joan McCarty (April 1993). Ronald Satchell was so involved in the Free Medical Clinic that he was nicknamed "Doc" Satchell. After nearly a year of planning and harassment by city officials, the clinic opened during the winter of 1969–1970.
9. Gray interview. See also interview with attorney Flint Taylor, November 1995, who provided volunteer legal assistance to the clinic.
10. *You've Got to Make a Commitment*, an uncopyrighted collection of Fred Hampton speeches printed in 1970.
11. *Chicago Defender*, October 6, 1969; *Chicago Daily News*, October 6, 1969.
12. *Chicago Defender*, October 7, 1969.
13. *Chicago Daily Defender*, October 14, 1969.
14. *Chicago Daily News*, October 10, 1969. Another eyewitness account of this shootout was later relayed to the author, though the source could not be verified; the author believes it may have been *Daily News* reporter Lu Palmer.
15. *Chicago Defender*, November 22 and November 28, 1969.
16. Ralph Knoohuizen et al., *Police and Their Use of Fatal Force in Chicago* (Chicago: Chicago Law Enforcement Study Group, 1972), 24–33.
17. *Chicago Journalism Review*, "What's It All About Eddie?," December 1972, 5–11.
18. Several former Panthers who wished to remain anonymous described these

events.

19. Hilliard, *This Side of Glory*, 112–123.

20. Brooks and Cook interviews.

21. *Chicago Sun-Times*, November 14, 1969.

22. *Chicago Defender*, November 22–28, 1969; *Chicago Sun-Times*, November 14, 1969; *Black Panther Community News Service*, December 1969; interviews with former Panthers Henry English, Lockett Dibbs, Bobby Rush, and others; and the author's own walkthrough of the crime scene conducted in 1979.

23. *Chicago Sun-Times*, November 14, 1969; *Chicago Tribune*, November 14, 1969.

24. Author's conjecture based on a walkthrough of the area approximately ten years after the incident.

25. *Chicago Sun-Times*, November 14, 1969.

26. *Appeals Brief*, FBI document produced by court order, Plaintiffs' Exhibit No. 43.

27. *Chicago Sun-Times*, May 16, 1970.

28. The only building that had a gangway leading to King Drive was the one Winters used that night. A local resident would have known this route. Once beyond the building he would have been outside the police perimeter and across a narrow street from a large wooded park. No helicopters were present, making escape possible.

29. *Chicago Sun-Times*, December 5, 1969.

30. I. Balbus, *The Dialectic of Legal Repression: Black Rebels Before the American Criminal Courts* (New York: Russell Sage Foundation, 1973), 167.

31. Dr. Edward Palmer related this incident at a fundraising event held in his honor in 1981. The author also heard Palmer recount the story shortly after Hampton's death, when Palmer began publishing his newspaper, *The Black X-Press*.

32. Interview with Leroy Martin, December 23, 1995; interview with James Brzeczek, April 1995.

33. *Brief for Plaintiff-Appellants Anderson, Bell, Clark, Satchell, and Truelock*, No. 77-1698, Appeals from the United States District Court for the Northern District of Illinois, Eastern Division, Appeal No. 70-C-1384, J. Sam Perry presiding, 15–18. This appeal followed the dismissal of the wrongful death suit against police officers involved in the raid that killed Fred Hampton. The brief draws heavily on government documents, including FBI records, to establish federal involvement. The appeal ultimately succeeded and the families of Fred Hampton and Mark Clark were awarded a settlement exceeding one million dollars. Hereafter cited as the *Appeals Brief*.

34. *Appeals Brief*, 26–28.

35. Kenneth O'Reilly, *Racial Matters: The FBI's Secret File on Black America, 1960–1972* (New York: Free Press, 1989), 314.

36. Ibid., 35–37.

37. *Appeals Brief,* 37–38.

38. *Appeals Brief,* 42.

39. Ibid., 35–42.

40. Ibid., 42.

41. A private autopsy requested by the Hampton family revealed the presence of secobarbital in Hampton's blood. This finding contradicted the official police autopsy. See the *Appeals Brief,* 112.

42. *Chicago Sun-Times,* December 5, 1969, lead story.

43. *Appeals Brief,* Trial Record (Tr.) 5051.

44. Ibid., 65, Tr. 9529.

45. Ibid., 69.

46. Executive Mandate No. 3 instructed all Panthers to respond to police raids with armed self-defense. See Huey P. Newton, *To Die for the People,* 11–13.

47. Interviews with Billy Brooks, Jewel Cook, and Willie Calvin (1983), and with Lynn French (1994).

48. Akua Njeri, *My Life with the Black Panther Party* (Chicago: Burning Spear Publications, 1991), 51–54. The author also worked with the Party in 1970 and found members generally suspicious of anyone who was not a Panther.

49. *Appeals Brief,* 14. William O'Neal's attempt to conduct a drug transaction by telephone from Panther headquarters was recorded by an FBI wiretap and reported to the Bureau. See FBI document PL #305, entered into evidence at trial.

50. *Chicago Sun-Times,* December 5, 1970; *The Black Panther,* January 12, 1970.

51. The author visited the office numerous times as a volunteer worker between 1972 and 1974; these observations are based on personal recollections from that period.

52. Many former Party members interviewed cited the transfer of personnel and resources to Oakland, California, as a major factor in the Illinois chapter's eventual dissolution. Interviewees included Akua Njeri (formerly Deborah Johnson), Yvonne King, Verlina Brewer, and Gregory Garrett.

53. Dunigan interview.

54. Interview with Jerry Dunigan, Danville Correctional Center, April 1994. Another witness to this account was Omie Daniels, a volunteer active in the Uptown community.

55. *People of the State of Illinois v. Jerry Dunigan,* No. 79-120, March 18, 1978, trial transcripts.

56. Interviews with Omie Daniels, Joan Auk, and Michael Thompson. Psychiatrist Tracey Good, also interviewed, believed Dunigan was suffering

from post-traumatic stress syndrome.

57. *People of the State of Illinois v. Jerry Dunigan*, trial record.

58. *Chicago Sun-Times*, August 4, 1970.

59. Interviews concerning Babatunde with Yvonne King (1983) and Bobby Rush (1983).

60. Henry English interview.

61. Yvonne King interview.

62. Frank Donner, *Protectors of Privilege: Red Squads and Police Repression in Urban America* (Berkeley: University of California Press, 1990), 101–150.

63. Author's personal experience living in the Austin neighborhood in 1974, when the Van-Central grocery store was converted into a liquor store.

64. Rally at the Center for Inner-City Studies, Oakwood Boulevard near Cottage Grove Avenue, winter 1970.

65. William Grimshaw, *Bitter Fruit: Black Politics and the Chicago Machine, 1931–1991* (Chicago: University of Chicago Press, 1992), 137.

66. After years of obstruction by Chicago political machine judge J. Sam Perry—who blocked attempts to indict State's Attorney Edward Hanrahan—the federal appeals court ultimately ruled in favor of the families of Fred Hampton and Mark Clark. The settlement followed one of the longest civil trials in Chicago history. See *Chicago Sun-Times*, January 14, 1984.

Chapter 7

Conclusion

In the forty years (1930-1970) of the radical left's involvement with Chicago's black community, there had been an appreciable increase in the political respect given to the black community. Between the years 1968 and 1974, the years that the Illinois Black Panther Party was the primary radical organization, there had also been both material gains and perhaps even spiritual gains. As one catalyst for these improvements, the Panther Party could take its share of the credit. As Herbert Haines notes in his book *Black Radicals and the Civil Rights Mainstream*, research indicates that increasing black radicalism in the sixties led to a willingness among funding sources to underwrite forms of black collective action that were more conservative.[1]

The Illinois Chapter of the Black Panther Party (the formal name of the Chicago chapter) provided that radical alternative, which made possible a dialogue on reform issues. There was a move to reform the police department, and despite the Chicago Police Department's resistance, a civilian review board was created.[2] Certainly, the Panther experience had plenty to do with that. In addition, the Panther Party's Free Breakfast for Children program had something to do with the state government's creation of a free lunch for children program. Moreover, it was in this period of time that open housing for Chicago's black people became a reality in most neighborhoods. The radical, confrontational methods of the Contract Buyers League, with whom the Panthers at times became involved, had tangible results on that housing issue.

The atmosphere in which these changes took place was one in which young people across the city, under the direction of the Illinois Black Panther Party, had formed a coalition of revolutionaries across ethnic lines. It is unlikely that the reality of a coalition of radical youth, citywide, did not influence the political and social atmosphere in which dialogue took place on that housing issue and other social issues.

Certainly, on a psychological level, very few black people had ever challenged a Chicago police officer, no matter how brutal he might have been. The Panthers confronted the police on the issue of police brutality, and that was an emotionally positive lift for poor people. It did not matter that the Panthers were struck down eventually. They had shown brutal police that they could expect armed resistance if they were excessive.

With the folding of the Illinois Black Panther Party, organized radicalism ceased to exist as a viable force in the black community. The old communists were just that, old and getting older, without attracting the youth, as they had in the 1930s, when they were the youth. Radical leftists still existed in black Chicago, but no longer did they have an organized presence there. Among the politically militant, the language of the left steadily gave way to the language of the cultural nationalists (the Black Panther term for them).

These cultural nationalists were economically conservative. The Reverend Al Sampson, for example, would ask black people to do business with Mobutu of Zaire in the name of racial unity.[3] The Panthers had called Mobutu a "pig," an enemy of the people. So the struggle for economic opportunities replaced the idea of a struggle for political rights and democracy for the poor.

The new black agenda was to expand economic opportunity for those who had a financial stake in the economic system. There was still talk of black unity, but it had an agenda that ignored the poor, at least as a collective entity.

Thus, it occurred that Jesse Jackson could push for more black school principals or more executives in the Pepsi Corporation and be perceived as militant (stubbornly insistent), but certainly not radical, because he did not challenge the way of organizing businesses; he simply wanted more black executives or more black contractors. This is a businessman's agenda.

Louis Farrakhan called for black businesses to make the black community independent, in what had most assuredly become, over the preceding decades, a more interdependent economic reality than ever before existed between black and white Americans. It would, therefore, seem that economic independence was not practical in post-Panther black communities.

The Black Panther Party had begun organizing the poor in the black community around the issue of class. They were consciously lower-class oriented, spoke of the masses, the lumpen, the people.[4] They spoke of a community agenda, demanding police controlled by the community, and of community institutions; economic, educational or health, which were accountable to the community. The people, the community mattered. The individual was not as important.[5] In the segregated reality of Chicago, their focus was necessarily poor, black people. However, their goal was to move from a unified community to act in alliance with other communities, to end capitalism and thereby end racism. Their ultimate goal was, therefore, the end of racism.[6] They believed that capitalism and racism were linked, and that the former *caused* the latter. The new agenda created by Ron Karenga and other nationalists focused on racism and based a unity on race, which did not aim to transcend racism (belief in race) but rather intended to take one "race" and remake it in an "African" image.[7]

Black oppression, these black particular nationalists believed, was unique. African Americans, according to nationalist spokesperson Leonard Jefferies, were unique "sun" people, who believed the spirit, as opposed to Europeans, who were "ice people," that is, egotistic and exploitative.[8] This exclusivity attitude promoted blacks doing business with blacks, perhaps, but had scant practical applications elsewhere. In fact, it alienated people in Chicago who otherwise had much in common with poor blacks in terms of economic woes. Even AIDS, according to Jefferies, was a conspiracy to destroy poor blacks.[9] The entire world was more integrated economically, socially and politically in 1980 than it had been in 1960, yet the post-Panther militants acted as if they could build a separate economy or live a separatist existence.

Leonard Jefferies, appointed head of black studies at CCNY, was evidently acceptable to the status quo, as was Ron Karenga. Karenga was, he said, attempting to bring an African culture to a people who had no culture(!)[10] It is, unmistakably, the backside of white racism, inculcated in Karenga's own mind, to have said that black Americans had no culture. A Klu Kluxer could not have said it better. It went right in the face of reason to even imply that a people who survived slavery, White Redemption, and the oppression of early 20th century America, had not formulated a quite powerful culture. Spokespersons like Karenga and Jefferies got the accolades of the 1980s militants. Unfortunately, no feasible political or social program could grow from so unrealistic a base. The Panthers had been naive, but they had been headed in a direction that had potential for real improvement in the lives of the poor. They began with the reality they perceived and offered a solution to the evils of that reality, to the oppression and repression of poor people.

Both the communists of the 1930s and 1940s and the Black Panther Party of the late 1960s and early 1970s addressed the issues of the poor. Both groups preached revolution and multiethnic alliances. Both groups originally were Marxist-based, but the Panther Party had shed its Marxism for a more home-grown radicalism, which made them something akin to the "Wobblies" of the early 20th century. Their leadership was not afraid of untried political theories, and they were not afraid of dealing with the economic and social woes with which the community's elected officials failed to deal. This was perhaps their primary attraction. They considered the lives of the people in their community and acted to change conditions for the majority of that community. Their actions were sometimes naive, often they were mistakes, but they were actions to which the powers that be had to respond. The Panther Party, in short, was the radical end of a community movement and challenged the status quo to develop some solutions to those very same social problems.

The Panther Party regarded the nationalists with suspicion. Recall Hampton's speech, "because they're constantly buying property within the system, and it's sort of hard for them to burn up Tuesday what they bought Monday."[11] The hierarchical nature of a competitive economic struggle on a level playing field, which the nationalists pushed for, has had little to do with improving the lives of everyday people. After all, if the extraordinary are rewarded without limits and the rest of the goodies are trickled down, no one average or below average in abilities (and most of us *are* average) is assured a share.

Even in a land of plenty, insecurity can abound, and it is in this economic insecurity that greed has its most favorable climate for growth. Now, in this insecure and competitive environment, if racism still flourishes, the successful members of the outcast race become targets of the less successful of the in-caste. Racism makes competition ultimately unfair. American history proves that this is so in numerous instances of wealthy blacks targeted for destruction. The Forten family and Jehu Jones of Charleston come immediately to mind as wealthy victims of white racism. In Chicago, the case of Chicago's first black bank owner, Jesse

142

Binga, was the same tragedy in 1932.[12] The Jones brothers, millionaire owners of policy wheels in Chicago, were similarly victimized by organized crime in the early 1950s, with the assistance of police officers. The Panthers offered a solution to that ultimate racist scenario in multiethnic cooperation and an end to racism. It is, unfortunately, a reality black and other nonwhite Americans must still come to terms with. How can successful black businesses survive in a competitive and racist society?

As a result of the revolutionary struggles of the 1960s and early 1970s, a better-armed police force was soon in place to handle the potential of violent revolution. While the reaction to Fred Hampton's assassination by police had produced a settlement of one and eight-tenths million dollars in compensation to Hampton's family, it had not gotten any of the police punished, nor punished any of the officials involved in planning this murder. That means the crime itself was implicitly approved. The message was unmistakable: they must pay for the murder of black radicals, but the assassins need not be punished. In fact, that monetary settlement began another, perhaps more deadly, pattern. Subsequent cases of proven police brutality, even murder, resulted in monetary compensation but little or no police being disciplined.[13] The city simply paid for the actions of police who were proven to be brutal. Getting a police officer convicted of police brutality was, by the 1990s, almost as hard as it had always been.[14] Furthermore, the new police superintendent soon defanged the review board.[15]

On a personal level, the Illinois Black Panther Party was a costly experience for the majority of members who had been dedicated to that Party. The Illinois Black Panther Party had excited its generation like nothing else before it. It had spawned the idea of a belief in the people and a willingness to serve the people. It was like a religion of the people. A few people came alive to that espoused potential of the people, and those who were so touched by the message of the Panther Party loved it, even if they never considered being Party members.[16]

Quite a few of the Party members and their families got hurt for that power of the spirit they had shown. In the possible contagion of that spirit of "we can do anything" was, perhaps, the fear that J. Edgar Hoover had of them. It was in their potential power to mobilize people outside of the economic and political framework on which the system ran. So these Panthers lost families, lost jobs, were sentenced to jail, were denied employment, for their potential, more so than anything they had accomplished. Scores of people had risked their future, if not their lives, to see children fed and given free medical care, while they recklessly threatened the federal government with revolution, while acting in ways that threatened the local Democratic Party. Some of them had come out of criminal activities and put their old ways down to serve their people. Some had come out of church-going families, or relocated Southern share-cropper families come north, simply poor, and without influence.

Once they got in trouble, they had no influential parent or friend to help them out. They were left to collect their lives as best they could. Subsequently, some ex-Panthers I interviewed or heard of were back into criminal activities. One, for example, was doing in 1979 what he had been doing before the Panthers were organized: pimping. He and his women were on Washington Street, setting a bad example for kids, not three blocks from where the Soto brothers were killed fighting for those kids.[17]

FBI informant O'Neal enticed two other Panthers into burglaries.[18] Another ex-Panther, from 1974 until the day he died, dependent on marijuana to help his glaucoma, burglarized to supply the drugs he needed, while living in squalor. Lockett Dibbs died in the mid-1980s, his spirit and his sacrifices long forgotten.[19] Brad Greene, a former Panther who had a four-year basketball scholarship to the University of Arizona, happened to be in the same car with a man who killed a Chicago police officer. He lost his scholarship and went to jail for the *crime* of being in the wrong place at the wrong time, and for being a member of the Black Panther Party. He came out of jail, several years later, a bitter man, committed a robbery and became a legitimate fugitive from the law. It was very hard to come out of the Illinois Black Panther Party, with the experiences of constant harassment by the authorities, the dirty tricks of the FBI, and the abuses people put on each other when they are under constant stress, and simply resume one's life. As Akua Njeri describes it in her booklet, *My Life in the Black Panther Party*, there were no social mechanisms for downloading the stress.

In 1974, after the destruction of the Panther Party, the former members either had to go along with society, accept it, become a spokesperson for it in order to survive, or become a semi-dropout, half-employed but withholding allegiance to the system. These hard choices added to the stress of a hostile power structure (police who had not forgotten, or maybe it just *seemed* that way) and raising a family could drive a person crazy, she explains.[20]

On the other hand, many Panthers used their experience to improve their lives, or at least were determined enough not to let it interfere with their lives. They run the gamut of professions, from landscape gardener, "Doc" Satchel (wounded five times by police in the December 4th raid), to government officials like Lynn French, Congressman Bobby Rush and Judge Cassandra Watson, actress Joan McCarty, dance director Joan Gray, and Boys Club counselor Billy Brooks. These people were the leaders of the Illinois Panthers. Their lives reflect the pain they experienced while showing the will and positive character to overcome it. They are strong people, leading purposeful lives, and they are the majority of the Illinois Black Panther Party who could be located. All of the twenty former Party members interviewed are quite proud of their experience in the Illinois Black Panther Party.

The radical left is ostensibly gone from the community. However, the black community has never quite fit into the categories of right and left. There have always been individuals who transcended these labels and simply worked for their community, theorizing about where they stood later. They were not afraid to work with Communists, Garveyites, Black Muslims or Panthers. The poor all over the world were, and continue to be, like this; if you offered them assistance, they would not ask, "Are you a leftist?" before they accepted your hand. Panther assistance, much like Communist assistance thirty years earlier, was accepted by default—no one else seemed to care.

Casting aside these traditional political labels, one could step back and look at the Panther movement in another light. Chicago's black community, and the culture its people have created, have been well adopted to the role it plays in Chicago society. The people are attuned to their roles by that culture they have created. Periodically, that culture may be designed to test the waters, to see if the majority culture is ready for class as well as racial integration into the life of the greater community. Maybe the Illinois Panthers were that test. Maybe "power to the people, off the pigs" really was a question that meant, are you going to accept me for who and what I am and allow me my right to live within the law, or kill me for the way I *talk* to you? Maybe the Panther experience nationwide was black American culture testing American democracy and finding out, by way of the Panthers, that democratic rights did not belong to the poor nonwhite. The culture of the black American has always shown that kind of resilience, and so perhaps the culture continued as it had, while there still remained that fertile ground for organizing the disorganized poor through serving the people.

There was not a need to kill 20-year-olds talking about revolution. However, when you fear the everyday people of any community so much you cannot get close to them, and when you lack the vision of the principles on which this country is founded, and are thereby not motivated to know everyday people, then you make mistakes. The history of the Illinois Black Panther Party is a history that highlighted these mistakes of the federal government, while exposing the undemocratic nature of local Chicago government, where the poor are concerned.

This brief episode of Chicago history is useful in that it contributes to an understanding of what American democracy was like for the poor of Chicago in the 1960s and before. In particular, how black Americans have lived in Chicago over the past half-century unfolds in that research. Clearly, for most black Chicagoans, traditional politics did not address the issues of their lives. Certainly, they suffered under a government that did not tolerate independent political thought. Although they did not suffer the humiliation of "whites only" signs, or being forced to sit on the back of the bus, as they had down South, they did suffer brutal police and intimidation, economic hardship and bad housing. Life for them was harsh and often brutal. They could not help but become so themselves. The history of the Illinois Panther Party illustrates that, historically speaking, there has been no democracy for the black poor in Chicago.

The Panther Party members faced the harshness and brutality head-on. They dreamed of a better life but lived squarely in the here and now. While they did not survive as an organization, they did, in their spirit, affirm their own belief in democracy. While the control institutions of the state wiped them out, those institutions were also forced to expose their undemocratic nature, and their powers were, temporarily at least, weakened in the process. The response to the manner in which the Illinois Panthers were eliminated was a powerful one.

The dumping of Edward Hanrahan by nonwhite voters, and the subsequent election of Harold Washington as the city's first black mayor, are usually connected to the assassination of Fred Hampton.[21] Hampton's assassination also forced the political system to be more circumspect. Perhaps the Panther Party made possible the success of the first black independent alderman on the West Side, Danny Davis. The price was high, but the governments were forced, for a time at least, to behave in a manner that respected the democratic rights that Americans profess. So perhaps the threat of a revolution is a necessary thing in our democracy. Certainly, our culture that espouses democracy nevertheless has withheld democracy from the poor, if we generalize from the black Chicago experience. Democracy is a risky venture in this country. If you wish to expound unpopular beliefs, particularly those that challenge the status quo, you are at risk. If the government tolerates that challenge, *it* is at risk. Eliminating that risk is easier. However, American democracy puts checks and balances on the branches of the government and has a bill of rights to force the government to allow that risk. That is what democracy means. Democracy means taking risks, letting people talk, even if you do not like what you hear. If the government had allowed the poor of Chicago to address the issues of their lives through the political arena, there would have been no Illinois Panther Party to begin with. The Illinois Panther Party arose out of that denial, *and* it was violently and illegally stamped out. That suppression created perhaps thousands of alienated people, having no desire to participate in the charade of a society claiming to be democratic and just. Many more episodes like this, and there would be no civic spirit in Chicago.

The principles America stands for, above and beyond making a dollar, the principles Americans want to be remembered in history for, I assume, are the principles of democracy. The Civil War was not fought so that capitalists could go on making money. At least we do not like to think that that was so, that all those soldiers died for the ascendancy of the almighty dollar. We like to believe that they died for a government of the people, by the people and for the people. The principles that Jefferson, Adams, Washington, Lincoln, Roosevelt, and La Follette lived by, we like to think, were the principles of democracy, one man, one vote.

Americans have considered themselves to be the city on a hill, which would show the world democracy can work. However, as Robert Taft once said, in order to export democracy, we must live democratically. America can win the hearts of the people of the world by living a democratic example.

If Americans do not live by that democratic principle, then what do they live by? Do Americans live simply to make money to have material things? Is real democracy a goal worth attaining? The challenge of the 1960s occurred when a youthful group of the outcast, who had never been a part of our nation's democracy, challenged the nation to let democracy work for them also. They did not do it nicely. Life had made them a hard people, and they put it to the nation in that hard way that bespoke who they were. They talked of revolution while strictly obeying the laws. They organized the unorganized poor. They attempted to do something like what the Populists of the late nineteenth century had tried before them. Those who rule shot them down rather efficiently, too efficiently for most of our good, because what they did to them, they can do to anyone.

Americans should not forget that. Revolution is a good thing, and power is a corrupting thing. One day, they will look back and treasure the spirit of revolution that surfaced in Chicago in 1969. It is a part of American heritage right out of 1776.

The black nationalists call the war on poor blacks genocide, but they have missed their mark. This nation needs a scapegoat, as long as it lets competition and greed go on without limits. So many Americans fail due to nothing less than our being average.

So they seem to need that scapegoat, and the poor, particularly those who dare to speak with honest disgust, are it. Americans also recognize the propensity of their government to make war on its own citizens when they espouse revolutionary doctrine, from the right or the left. The last thing most Americans want is for the current scapegoat to be wiped out, for then there would be a new scapegoat–which there may well be anyway–looking at more recent attacks on the radical right. Once the radical right is wiped out, then perhaps the liberals become a target. So, the tear in the fabric, the illegal destruction of one group, can lead to the destruction of the entire cloth. In the life of our nation and the city of Chicago, this episode is, therefore, one of which every citizen should be aware.

Notes

1. Herbert Haines, *Black Radicals and the Civil Rights Mainstream, 1954–1970* (Knoxville: University of Tennessee Press, 1988), 173.

2. Janice Bauer, "The Chicago Police Department Office of Professional Standards: A One-Year Analysis," Chicago Law Enforcement Study Group (CLEGS), 1976, 7–13. This report, along with an interview with attorney Flint Taylor of the People's Law Office, indicates that the Civilian Review Board has historically been dominated by individuals connected with the police, and that its recommendations must be approved by the police superintendent. Despite its limited authority, the board's existence has been consistently opposed by the Confederation of Police, the officers' fraternal organization.

3. Rev. Al Sampson, remarks at the Second Annual Black Leadership Conference, Northern Illinois University, April 1994. Recordings held by the Northern Illinois University Black Studies Center.

4. Huey P. Newton, *To Die for the People* (San Francisco: Writers and Readers Publishing, 1973), 55–59.

5. Ibid., 110.

6. Newton, *To Die for the People*, 192–193.

7. Floyd B. Barbour, ed., *The Black Power Revolt: A Collection of Essays* (Boston: Porter Sargent, 1968), "The Quotable Karenga," 165–167.

8. In Chicago, Rev. Al Sampson of Fernwood United Methodist Church and Professor Robert Starks of the Center for Inner-City Studies often refer to the unique oppression experienced by African Americans. The point being made here is that statements framed in this way can unintentionally alienate other groups who may argue that their own historical suffering was comparable or greater. For example, Kurds in Iran during the 1990s or the Sioux in South Dakota in 1900 might argue their oppression was more severe. Such framing can therefore complicate coalition building.

9. *New York Magazine*, June 7, 1993, 46.

10. Barbour, *The Black Power Revolt*, 166.

11. *Vita Wa Watu*, 11.

12. Clarence Darrow, representing banker Jesse Binga, argued that Binga was prosecuted for actions that were common practice among white businessmen in Chicago.

13. "Cop's Free Rein Costs City Millions: Police Rarely Punished Over Repeated Misconduct Suits," *Chicago Sun-Times*, January 8, 1995, 1.

14. Flint Taylor interview. Taylor, of the People's Law Office, which handles numerous police brutality cases, estimated that convictions against police officers occur in roughly 5 percent of cases today; historically the rate was

closer to 2 percent.

15. CLEGS report cited above, 13.

16. Nearly every community activist interviewed expressed admiration for the Illinois Black Panther Party, including James Montgomery, Nancy Jefferson, Richard Barnett, Edward Crawford, Robert Lucas, Lucy Montgomery, Patricia Berg, Bernetta Howell, Danny Davis, Howard Saffold, Renault Robinson, Edward "Buzz" Palmer, and Illinois State Representative Alice Palmer. Among many residents of Chicago's Black communities, the author reports hearing little criticism of the Panthers except during the period when the organization was active, when numerous defamatory rumors circulated.

17. Interview with Henry English and Willie Calvin, April 1981.

18. Former Chicago Police Superintendent James Brzeczek asserted that the Panthers included a criminal element. Subsequent research suggests that some criminal activity was present; however, much of it appears to have centered around FBI informant William O'Neal, which has influenced the author's interpretation of these claims.

19. The author maintained contact with Lockett "Lucky" Dibbs for approximately a decade after the initial interview; this statement reflects those ongoing conversations.

20. Akua Njeri, *My Life with the Black Panther Party* (Chicago: Burning Spear Publications, 1991), 45–49.

21. David Fremon, *Chicago Politics: Ward by Ward* (Bloomington: Indiana University Press, 1988), 137.

Bibliography

Primary Sources

Interviews

Abrons, JoNina. Former member, Detroit Black Panther Party. Personal interview, March 26, 1996.

Barnett, Richard. Community political activist, North Lawndale community, Chicago. Personal interviews, July 21, 1993, and August 4, 1993.

Barrett, Bernetta Howell. Former aldermanic candidate, 25th Ward. Personal interview, April 30, 1994.

Berg, Patricia. Founder of the National Black Draft Counselors (1970) and former president of Chicago SNCC. Personal interview, May 11, 1995.

Brzeczek, Richard. Former superintendent, Chicago Police Department (1980–1983). Telephone interview, February 26, 1996.

Brooks, Billy Lamar. Former deputy minister of education, Illinois Black Panther Party. Personal interviews, April 11–13, 1996.

Calvin, Willie. Former member, Illinois Black Panther Party. Personal interviews, August 13–14, 1981.

Cincotta, Gail. Former president, Organization for a Better Austin, a West Side community organization and housing advocacy group.

Personal interview, February 19, 1995.

Cook, Cleveland. Former member, Illinois Black Panther Party. Personal interviews, September 1981 and October 18, 1996.

Cook, Jewel. Former field lieutenant, Illinois Black Panther Party. Personal interviews, October 9, 1981, and July 18, 1983.

Crawford, Edward "Fats." Founder of the Deacons for Defense and later of the National Negro Rifle Association. Personal interviews, April 12, 1981, and August 9, 1981.

Cullinan, Jones (formerly Joan Auk). Co-director of the film *The Murder of Fred Hampton*. Personal interview, August 29, 1994.

Daniels, Omie. Former activist volunteer with the Illinois Black Panther Party and film assistant in the filming of *American Revolution II* and *The Murder of Fred Hampton*. Personal interviews, August 17–18, 1994.

Davis, Corneal. Retired state legislator and political activist in Chicago during the 1930s. Personal interview, July 12, 1992.

Davis, Danny. Second elected independent Black alderman on Chicago's West Side after Ben Lewis and currently U.S. congressman. Personal interview, October 13, 1994.

Dibbs, Lockett. Former member, Illinois Black Panther Party. Personal interviews, September 11, 1981, and July 3, 1984.

Dunigan, Jerry. Former member, Illinois Black Panther Party; badly victimized by COINTELPRO. His wife was killed in the machinations of William O'Neal, the FBI's agent provocateur in the Illinois Black Panther Party. Personal interview, May 1993.

English, Henry. Former member, Illinois Black Panther Party and former student president at Malcolm X City College. Personal interview, August 11, 1981.

Finke, David. Quaker activist and civil rights marcher in the Dr. King–led march into Marquette Park for open housing. Personal interview, March 14, 1982.

Flores, Carlos. Former leader in the Young Lords. Personal interview, January 17, 1996.

Flory, Ishmael. Former member, Communist Party, and secretary of the National Negro Congress in the late 1940s. Personal interviews, October 18, 1992, and October 24, 1992.

French, Lynn. Former member, Illinois Black Panther Party. Personal interview, March 16, 1994.

Garrett, Gregory. Former member, Illinois Black Panther Party. Personal interview, October 5, 1978.

Gray, Joan. Former field lieutenant, Illinois Black Panther Party. Personal interview, September 17, 1996.

Jackson, Marianne. Attorney for member of the Main 21, El Rukns. Personal interview, April 4, 1993.

James, Michael. Founder of Rising Up Angry. Personal interview, February 6, 1996.

Jefferson, Nancy. President of the Midwest Community Council and president of the Civilian Police Review Board. Personal interviews, June 30, 1981, and September 13, 1984.

Jones, Sydney. Retired Cook County judge and former activist in Third Ward aldermanic politics. Personal interview, July 13, 1992.

King, Yvonne. Former deputy minister of labor, Illinois Black Panther Party. Personal interviews, August 1–2, 1981.

Kuttner, Peter. Former member of Rising Up Angry (RUA). Personal interview, June 4, 1993.

McCarty, Joan. Former member, Illinois Black Panther Party. Personal interviews, July 4, 1985, and July 21, 1994.

Martin, Leroy. Retired superintendent of the Chicago Police Department. Personal interview, December 24, 1994.

Montgomery, James. Attorney who defended several Black Panthers involved in the misnamed "shootout" with police on December 4, 1969. Personal interview, July 3, 1982.

Montgomery, Lucille. Donor for several community service programs involving the civil rights movement. Personal interview, July 16, 1981.

Palmer, Edward "Abuzz." Founder of the Afro-American Patrolmen's

League. Personal interview, September 12, 1984.

Pennington, Ben Akalomo. Former member, Illinois Black Panther Party. Personal interview, October 3, 1983.

Peery, Nelson. Former member, Communist Labor Party and author of *Black Fire: The Story of an American Revolutionary*. Personal interview, April 13, 1994.

Pincham, Eugene. Retired judge and founder of the Harold Washington Party; also defended Edward Crawford as an attorney in 1968. Personal interview, August 19, 1992.

Rahman, Ahmad. Former member, Illinois Black Panther Party. Personal interview, March 28, 1996.

Reese, Harry. Precinct captain, 29th Ward Peoples' Assembly; longtime political activist on Chicago's West Side associated with Congressman Danny Davis's organization. Personal interview, November 20, 1994.

Robinson, Renault. Founder of the Afro-American Patrolmen's League. Personal interview, August 15, 1983.

Rush, Bobby L. Former deputy minister of defense, Illinois Black Panther Party, and currently U.S. congressman for the South Side of Chicago. Personal interview, April 5, 1982.

Saffold, Howard. Former member of the Afro-American Patrolmen's League. Personal interview, August 11, 1982.

South, Wesley. Radio talk show host, WVON 1390; also ran for alderman on an independent ticket on the West Side in the early 1960s. Personal interview, August 3, 1993.

Sykes, George. Unitarian minister involved in the open housing marches with Dr. King into the Marquette Park and Gage Park neighborhoods. Personal interview, June 16, 1987.

Taylor, Flint. Attorney for the survivors of the police raid of December 4, 1969, which killed Panther leader Fred Hampton. Personal interview, November 1, 1994.

Thomas, Floyd. Aldermanic candidate in the 29th Ward in 1994 and former member of the Deacons for Defense and Justice. Personal interview, November 20, 1994.

Collected Papers

The Papers of Claude Barnett. Chicago Historical Society. Barnett was the founder and director of the Associated Negro Press, which collected newspaper articles about Black Americans printed in Black daily newspapers from the 1920s through the 1960s.

The Papers of Archibald Carey Jr. Chicago Historical Society. Carey was a former Republican alderman of Chicago's 3rd Ward.

The Papers of Earl B. Dickerson. Chicago Historical Society. Dickerson served as alderman of Chicago's 2nd Ward and ran for Congress during the 1940s but was defeated by William Dawson.

The Papers of Claude Lightfoot. DuSable Museum. Lightfoot was a member of the Illinois Communist Party.

The Papers of Lucille Montgomery. DuSable Museum. Montgomery was a benefactor of several politically radical activist groups during the 1960s and 1970s.

Government and Other Official Documents

U.S. Congress. Senate. Senate Report No. 94-755, *Intelligence Activities and the Rights of Americans*, Book II. Committee on Intelligence Activities, Senator Frank Church, chairman. 94th Cong., 2nd sess.

U.S. Congress. Senate. Senate Report No. 94-755, *Supplemental Detailed Staff Reports on Intelligence Activities and the Rights of Americans*, Book III. 94th Cong., 2nd sess.

Brief for Plaintiff-Appellants Anderson, Bell, Clark, Stachell, and Truelock. No. 77-1698. Appeals from the U.S. District Court for the Northern District of Illinois, Eastern Division, Appeal No. 70-C-1384, J. Sam Perry, judge.

State of Illinois Senate Legislative Hearings on Police Brutality. Senator Richard Newhouse presiding. Summer 1969. Audio tapes.

Newspapers

The Black Panther Community News. July 5, 1969; July 12, 1969; July 19, 1969; August 23, 1969; November 13, 1969; February 13, 1970; March 12, 1977.

The Chicago American. June 12, 1966.

The Chicago Daily Defender and *The Chicago Defender.* April 6, 1926; March 15, 1930; March 28, 1931; August 8, 1931; January 16, 1932; July 8, 1939; May 22, 1943; March 5–10, 1958; July 10, 1967; November 1, 1967; May 1, 1969; May 6–8, 1969; May 13–15, 1969; May 20, 1969; June 5, 1969; July 1, 1969; July 2–3, 1969; July 7–9, 1969; July 17, 1969; July 23, 1969; October 7, 1969; November 22, 1969. "Two Police Slain in Battle." November 28, 1969; December 13–14, 1969.

The Chicago Daily News. "A Panther–Police Gun Battle." August 1, 1969. October 6, 1969; October 7, 1969; October 15, 1969; July 20, 1970; July 25–26, 1970; July 30, 1970.

The Chicago Sun-Times. "Klansmen in Chicago Police Department." December 28–29, 1967; January 3, 1968; April 1, 1968; April 3–5, 1968; November 11, 1968; April 10, 1969; April 15, 1969; April 23, 1969; June 4–5, 1969; July 16, 1969; August 1, 1969; October 6, 1969; October 13, 1969; November 13, 1969; December 5, 1969. "Nightmare to Reality: How Brothers Died in Ghetto." March 2, 1970; May 4–5, 1970; May 16, 1970; June 18, 1970; October 18, 1970; October 24, 1972; December 1, 1973; December 11, 1973; December 24, 1974; March 20, 1977; January 30, 1978; September 2, 1978; January 17, 1990; January 8, 1995.

The Chicago Tribune. April 3, 1955; June 2, 1969; November 24, 1969; November 29, 1974; January 22, 1978; January 30, 1978.

The Chicago Reader. "The Last Hours of William O'Neal." January 26, 1990.

The New York Times. "Civil Rights Marchers in Chicago." October 23, 1963. "Chicago 2nd School Boycott." February 6, 1964. "Marchers at Chicago City Hall." July 1, 1965. July 22, 1965; January 2, 1966; March 17, 1966; June 13, 1966; August 13, 1966; January 16, 1967; December 29, 1967; January 11, 1968; July 6, 1970; July 8, 1970; August 16–18, 1970.

Chicago Whip. October 1, 1921.

Muhammad Speaks. "The Death of Ben Lewis." April 1, 1963.

Peoria Journal Star. "Mark Clark Slain in Chicago, Guilty Here." February 18, 1990.

Autobiographies

Brown, Elaine. *A Taste of Power: A Black Woman's Story.* New York: Pantheon, 1993.

Brown, H. Rap. *Die Nigger, Die!* New York: Dial Press, 1970.

Hilliard, David. *This Side of Glory: The Autobiography of David Hilliard and the Story of the Black Panther Party.* New York: Little, Brown, 1993.

Malcolm X. *The Autobiography of Malcolm X.* New York: Grove Press, 1964.

Secondary Sources

Books

Alinsky, Saul. *Radicals in Urban Politics: The Alinsky Approach.* Chicago: University of Chicago Press, 1974.

Aminah, Beverly McCloud. *African American Islam.* New York: Routledge, 1995.

Arden, Mark. *An American Verdict.* New York: Doubleday, 1973.

Anderson, Alan, and George Pickering. *Confronting the Color Line: The Broken Promises of the Civil Rights Movement in Chicago.* Athens: University of Georgia Press, 1986.

Balbus, Isaac. *The Dialectic of Legal Repression: Black Rebels before the American Criminal Courts.* New York: Russell Sage Foundation, 1973.

Barbour, Floyd. *The Black Power Revolt: A Collection of Essays.* Boston: South End Press, 1968.

Baruch, Roger-M., and Peggy Jones. *The Vanguard: A Photographic Essay on the Black Panthers.* Boston: Beacon Press, 1970.

Barrett, James. *Work and Community in the Jungle: Chicago's Packinghouse Workers, 1894–1922.* Urbana: University of Illinois Press, 1987.

Breitman, George, ed. *Malcolm X Speaks: Selected Speeches and Statements.* New York: Grove Press, 1966.

Carson, Clayborne. *In Struggle: SNCC and the Black Awakening of the 1960s.* Cambridge: Harvard University Press, 1981.

Cayton, Horace R., and St. Clair Drake. *Black Metropolis: A Study of Negro Life in a Northern City.* New York: Harcourt, Brace, 1945.

Chicago Commission on Race Relations. *The Negro in Chicago: A Study of Race Relations and a Race Riot.* Chicago: University of Chicago Press, 1922.

Chevigny, Paul. *Police Power.* New York: Pantheon, 1969.

Chicago Factbook Consortium, eds. *Local Community Fact Book: Chicago Metropolitan Area, 1960, 1970, and 1980.* Chicago: University of Illinois at Chicago, 1983.

Churchill, Ward, and Jim Vander Wall. *Agents of Repression: The FBI's Secret Wars against the Black Panther Party and the American Indian Movement.* Boston: South End Press, 1990.

Cleaver, Eldridge. *Soul on Ice.* New York: Dell, 1968.

Conot, Robert. *Rivers of Blood, Years of Darkness.* New York: Morrow, 1968.

Cruse, Harold. *The Crisis of the Negro Intellectual.* Chicago: University of Chicago Press, 1970.

Currie, Elliott, and Jerome Skolnick. *Crisis in American Institutions.* New York: Little, Brown, 1974.

Davis, Angela, and Bettina Aptheker, eds. *If They Come in the Morning.* New York: New American Library, 1971.

DeMaris, Ovid. *Captive City: Chicago in Chains.* New York: Lyle Stuart, 1969.

Donner, Frank. *Protectors of Privilege: Red Squads and Police Repression in Urban America.* Berkeley: University of California Press, 1990.

Duncan, Beverly, and Otis Dudley Duncan. *The Negro Population in Chicago.* Chicago: University of Chicago Press, 1957.

Eliff, John. *Reform of FBI Intelligence Operations.* Princeton: Princeton

University Press, 1979.

Fanon, Frantz. *The Wretched of the Earth.* New York: Grove Press, 1963.

Frazier, E. Franklin. *Black Bourgeoisie.* Chicago: University of Chicago Press, 1959.

Fremon, David. *Chicago Politics, Ward by Ward.* Bloomington: Indiana University Press, 1988.

Fish, John. *Black Power/White Control: The Struggle of the Woodlawn Organization in Chicago.* Princeton: Princeton University Press, 1973.

Foner, Philip S. *The Black Panthers Speak.* New York: J. B. Lippincott, 1970.

Fry, Joseph B. *Locked Out Americans: A Memoir.* New York: Harper and Row, 1974.

Glick, Brian. *War at Home: Covert Action against U.S. Activists and What We Can Do About It.* Boston: South End Press, 1988.

Goldsmith, Andrew, and John Goldsmith, eds. *The Police Community: Dimensions of an Occupational Subculture.* Pacific Palisades, CA: Palisades Publishers, 1975.

Gosnell, Harold F. *Negro Politicians: The Rise of Negro Politics in Chicago.* Chicago: University of Chicago Press, 1967.

Grier, William H., and Price M. Cobbs. *Black Rage.* New York: Basic Books, 1968.

Grimshaw, William. *Bitter Fruit: Black Politics and the Chicago Machine, 1931–1991.* Chicago: University of Chicago Press, 1992.

Haines, Herbert H. *Black Radicals and the Civil Rights Mainstream, 1954–1970.* Knoxville: University of Tennessee Press, 1988.

Haywood, Harry. *Black Bolshevik: Autobiography of an Afro-American Communist.* New York: International Publishers, 1978.

Heath, G. Louis. *Off the Pigs!: The History and Literature of the Black Panther Party.* Metuchen, NJ: Scarecrow Press, 1976.

Hilliard, David. *This Side of Glory: The Autobiography of David Hilliard and the Story of the Black Panther Party.* New York: Little, Brown, 1993.

Hirsch, Arnold R. *Making the Second Ghetto: Race and Housing in Chicago, 1940–1960.* Chicago: University of Chicago Press, 1983.

Holli, Melvin G., and Paul M. Green. *The Making of the Mayor: Chicago, 1983.* Grand Rapids, MI: Eerdmans, 1984.

hooks, bell. *Killing Rage: Ending Racism.* New York: Henry Holt, 1995.

Horne, Gerald. *Black and Red: W. E. B. Du Bois and the Afro-American Response to the Cold War, 1944–1963.* Albany: State University of New York Press, 1986.

Kardiner, Abram, and Lionel Ovesey. *The Mark of Oppression: Explorations in the Personality of the American Negro.* New York: Knopf, 1951.

Keiser, Robert L. *Vice Lords: Warriors of the Streets.* New York: Holt, Rinehart and Winston, 1969.

King, Martin Luther, Jr. *Where Do We Go from Here: Chaos or Community?* Boston: Beacon Press, 1967.

Kitagawa, Evelyn M., and Karl E. Taueber. *Local Community Fact Book for the Chicago Metropolitan Area, 1980.* Chicago: University of Chicago Press, 1983.

Knauss, Peter. *Chicago: A One-Party State.* Chicago: University of Illinois Press, 1983.

Knoohuizen, Richard, et al. *Police and Their Fatal Use of Force in Chicago.* Chicago: Chicago Law Enforcement Study Group, 1972.

Lait, Jack, and Lee Mortimer. *Chicago Confidential.* New York: Avon Books, 1950.

Lasch, Christopher. *The Agony of the American Left.* New York: Knopf, 1969.

Lindberg, Richard. *To Serve and Collect: Chicago Politics and Police Corruption from the Lager Beer Riot to the Summerdale Scandal.* New York: Praeger, 1991.

Logan, Rayford W., and Michael R. Winston, eds. *Dictionary of American Negro Biography.* New York: Norton, 1982.

Malcolm X. *The Autobiography of Malcolm X.* New York: Grove Press, 1964.

Mao Tse-tung. *Quotations from Chairman Mao Tse-tung.* Peking: Foreign Languages Press, 1967.

Marable, Manning. *Black American Politics: From the Washington Marches to Jesse Jackson.* London: New Left Books, 1985.

Marine, Gene. *The Black Panthers.* New York: New American Library, 1969.

McClory, William A. *The Black Presence in the Bible.* Chicago: Black Light Fellowship, 1995.

Meyer, Harold M., and Richard C. Wade. *Chicago: The Growth of a Metropolis.* Chicago: University of Chicago Press, 1969.

Millea, Thomas. *Ghetto Fever.* Milwaukee: Bruce Publishing Company, 1968.

Naison, Mark. *Communists in Harlem during the Depression.* New York: Grove Press, 1983.

Newton, Huey P. *To Die for the People: The Writings of Huey P. Newton.* New York: Random House, 1972.

Njeri, Akinyele Omowale. *My Life with the Black Panther Party.* Chicago: Burning Spear Publications, 1991.

O'Connor, Len. *Clout: Mayor Daley and His City.* New York: Avon Books, 1975.

Ottley, Roi. *The Lonely Warrior: The Life and Times of Robert S. Abbott.* New York: Henry Regnery, 1955.

Ovesey, Lionel, and Abram Kardiner. *The Mark of Oppression: Explorations in the Personality of the American Negro.* Cleveland: World Publishing Company, 1951.

Pearson, Hugh. *Shadow of the Panther: Huey Newton and the Price of Black Power in America.* Reading, MA: Addison-Wesley, 1994.

Pinderhughes, Dianne M. *Race and Ethnicity in Chicago Politics.* Chicago: University of Illinois Press, 1987.

Powers, Richard Gid. *Secrecy and Power: The Life of J. Edgar Hoover.* New York: Free Press, 1987.

Rakove, Milton L. *Don't Make No Waves... Don't Back No Losers.*

Bloomington: Indiana University Press, 1975.

Ralph, James R., Jr. *Northern Protest: Martin Luther King, Jr., Chicago, and the Civil Rights Movement.* Cambridge, MA: Harvard University Press, 1993.

Reilly, O. K. *Racial Matters: The FBI's Secret File on Black America, 1960–1972.* New York: Free Press, 1989.

Robinson, Samuel J. *The Badge: They Are Trying to Bury Me.* Monticello, UT: Simon Belt Publishers, 1975.

Roemer, William F., Jr. *Man Against the Mob: The Inside Story of How the FBI Cracked the Chicago Mob by the Agent Who Led the Attack.* New York: Ivy Books, 1989.

Seale, Bobby. *Seize the Time: The Story of the Black Panther Party and Huey P. Newton.* New York: Random House, 1970.

Skolnick, Jerome H. *The Politics of Protest.* New York: Simon & Schuster, 1969.

Spears, Allen J. *Black Chicago: The Making of a Negro Ghetto.* Chicago: University of Chicago Press, 1967.

Summers, A. *Official and Confidential: The Secret Life of J. Edgar Hoover.* New York: G. P. Putnam's Sons, 1993.

Theoharis, A., and J. Cox. *The Boss: J. Edgar Hoover and the Great American Inquisition.* Philadelphia: Temple University Press, 1988.

Travis, D. *An Autobiography of Black Chicago.* Chicago: Urban Research Institute, 1983.

Tuttle, W. *Race Riot: Chicago in the Red Summer of 1919.* New York: Atheneum, 1974.

Van Deburg, W. *New Day in Babylon: The Black Power Movement and American Culture, 1965–1975.* Chicago: University of Chicago Press, 1992.

Wade, R., and A. Meier. *Chicago: Growth of a Metropolis.* Chicago: University of Chicago Press, 1972.

Waldrop, F. *McCormick of Chicago.* New York: Prentice Hall, 1966.

Wilson, W. J. *The Declining Significance of Race: Blacks and Changing*

American Institutions. Chicago: University of Chicago Press, 1983.

Wintersmith, R. *Police and the Black Community*. New York: D.C. Heath, 1974.

Unpublished Sources

Jefferson, Alphine. *Housing Discrimination and Community Response in North Lawndale (Chicago), 1948–1968*. PhD diss., Duke University, 1979.

Newton, Huey P. *War Against the Panthers: A Study of Repression in America*. PhD diss., University of California, Santa Cruz, 1980.

Willis, D. J. *Critical Analysis of Mass Political Education and Community Organization as Utilized by the Black Panther Party*. PhD diss., University of Massachusetts, 1976.

Reid, Christopher Robert. *A Study of Black Politics and Protest in Depression-Decade Chicago*. PhD diss., Kent State University, 1982.

You've Got to Make a Commitment. Booklet of Fred Hampton speeches, 1972.

Periodicals

The Atlantic Monthly. "Alone in Cover-Up Country." Vol. 232, October 1973.

Chicago Journalism Review. "What's It All About, Eddie?" December 1972.

Chicago Journalism Review. "Editorials on Race, 1954–1968." August 1972.

Ebony. "The Gang Phenomenon: Big City Headache." Vol. 22, no. 10, August 1967.

Ebony. "Black Panthers: Huey P. Newton." Vol. 24, August 1969.

Journal of American History. Gordon, Rita. "Change in the Political Alignment of Chicago's Negroes during the New Deal." Vol. 56, December 1969.

Journal of Negro History. "Jesse Binga." January 1973.

The Nation. "Out to Get the Panthers: FBI and the Chicago Police." Vol. 209, July 28, 1969.

The New Yorker. "A Reporter at Large: The Panthers and the Police—A Pattern of Genocide." February 13, 1971.

Newsweek. "Converting a Gang into Organization Men." Vol. 69, June 5, 1967.

Newsweek. "Opportunity, Please Knock Chorus." Vol. 70, February 5, 1968.

Newsweek. "Panther Hunt." Vol. 71, April 22, 1968.

Newsweek. "Reforming Street Gangs." Vol. 72, July 15, 1968.

Newsweek. "On the Prowl." Vol. 72, September 23, 1968.

Newsweek. "Radicals: Black Panthers in the Vanguard." Vol. 74, August 4, 1969.

Newsweek. "Shoot It Out." Vol. 74, December 15, 1969.

Newsweek. "Too Late for Panthers." Vol. 74, 1970.

Newsweek. "Controversial Verdict." Vol. 75, February 2, 1970.

Newsweek. "Slap on the Wrist." Vol. 75, May 25, 1970.

Newsweek. "Philadelphia Guerrilla War." Vol. 76, September 14, 1970.

Newsweek. "Double-Agent: Thirteen Harlem Black Panthers on Trial." Vol. 76, November 23, 1970.

Newsweek. "Panther Ghost." Vol. 78, September 14, 1970.

Review of Radical Political Economics. Manning, M. "Black Power in Chicago." Vol. 17, 1985.

Time. "Chicago Gang War." Vol. 92, July 5, 1968.

Time. "Police and Panthers at War." Vol. 94, December 12, 1969.

Time. "Panthers' Honky Lawyer." Vol. 95, January 12, 1970.

Time. "The Divided Panthers." Vol. 97, February 22, 1971.

Time. "Verdict for Fast Eddie." Vol. 100, November 6, 1972.

U.S. News & World Report. "Invasion by Armed Black Panthers, Sacramento, California." Vol. 62, May 15, 1967.

U.S. News & World Report. "We're Going to Shoot the Cops." Vol. 63, May 29, 1967.

Vita Wa Watu: A New African Theoretical Journal. "Fred Hampton Speech." Winter 1989.

About the Author

Historian Jon F. Rice is a retired educator, first-person historical interpreter, and artist. The middle child of Chicago parents, Rice has spent much of his life studying and interpreting Chicago's history and its communities. His extensive research and first-hand documentation on the Illinois Chapter of the Black Panther Party have been a vital resource for historians, students, and books and films.

Over the course of his career, he taught in Chicago Public Schools, San Diego Unified School District, and the Illinois Department of Corrections, Juvenile Division. He also served as an adjunct professor of history at Roosevelt University, Aurora College, and the University of Massachusetts Boston. Rice earned a Ph.D. in American History from Northern Illinois University and studied environmental chemistry at the University of Illinois at Chicago. In addition to his academic work, he has long been active as a first-person historical interpreter, portraying figures such as Crispus Attucks; a Pilgrim at Plimoth Patuxet; an African American Civil War veteran; and a Wampanoag elder.

Throughout his career, Rice has been active in community and political organizing, including service with the Illinois Black Panther Party (1969–1974), the Southeast Side Environmental Task Force, and People for Community Recovery in Altgeld Gardens. He lives in Chicago with his family and continues to write stories and perform historical interpretations in Pembroke, Illinois.